CONTENTS

CREATE YOUR OWN
SCRAPBOOK

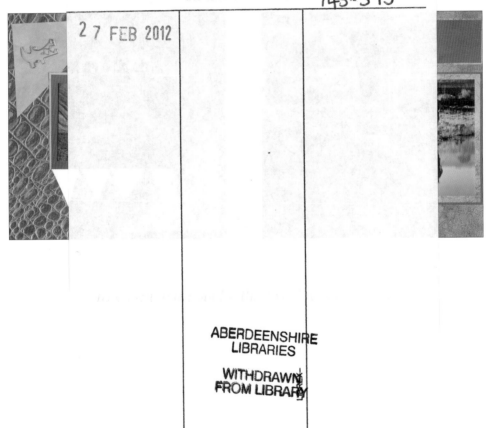
ANNAMÈ WOLMARANS

TECHNIQUES 69

BASICS

WHAT IS SCRAPBOOKING?

Scrapbooking is an art form by which means photographs and other mementoes are preserved in an acid-free environment in the most interesting way possible. Keeping the environment acid free ensures that the photos will not discolour or disintegrate. The art of scrapbooking is loads of fun and will ensure that your memories are transferred from the photo box to the photo album.

And that brings us to the reason why you're going to love learning this hobby, and why it's so addictive: by preserving your photos in an acid-free environment, where they are protected from damage and the ravages of time, you are creating an heirloom for your family, safeguarding a part of your life for your children's children. You're telling your life story so that generations to come will be able to see how you lived, what you looked like, and come to know what was important to you and everything you experienced in your lifetime. In this way you'll be providing a record of yourself and your family for posterity so that you won't just be an unknown face on a photo in a box on a cupboard shelf, but be part of your descendants' lives.

There are a few basic principles you should follow when practising the art of scrapbooking, but these are merely guidelines, since everyone's style and techniques differ. It's important to remember that you can't make a mistake in scrapbooking; there is no right or wrong way – only creative fun. All you need to do is to tell your story, and enjoy telling it.

BASIC EQUIPMENT

Because scrapbooking has become popular as a hobby mainly in the USA and developed into a fully-fledged art form, many products are imported and therefore cost a little more than you might expect. Fortunately scrapbooking has taken off so well in many other countries that local manufacturers are starting to produce some of the products needed for this hobby.

Before starting, however, you'll need to acquire these basic necessities:

PAPER

Locally manufactured paper is available as well as paper imported from Australia and the USA. Paper comes in two sizes, namely 8½ x 11 inch (21.59 x 27.94 cm), or the more popular 12 x 12 inch (30.48 x 30.48 cm) size.

A great variety of paper can be used for scrapbooking – ordinary white or coloured paper, as well as variegated paper and paper with definite patterns and themes. There is also vellum paper, transparent and almost like plastic, used mostly when you want the background to show through. Handmade paper is very attractive and makes interesting frayed edges when torn. I also like to work with embossed paper and paper with a velvety finish.

Paper must always be acid free. Make sure you don't use handmade kinds that are made from paper that isn't acid free, because the end product would of course not be acid free. The bonding agent added when paper is manufactured sometimes contains acid.

Handmade paper that is usually safe is mulberry paper. Some kinds of decoupage paper are also acid free. The easiest way to test whether paper is safe for scrapbooking is to use an acid-testing pen. Most craft shops have two kinds and both work well. Read the instructions on the pen to find out how to test for acid in paper.

The various kinds of scrapbooking paper available

GLUE

The most important kind of adhesive you should obtain is photo splits. At present photo splits are still only manufactured in the USA, Germany and Australia, and any of these can be used. The less expensive kinds are available in boxes, whereas the more expensive ones come in a plastic container for which refills can be purchased.

You'll also need to buy a glue stick. Make sure it specifically states on the container or packaging that it is acid free, and not just safe to use. PowerPritt® is freely available and any of the imported sticks can be purchased.

You'll also require wet glue, which is basically liquid glue with which to stick embellishments like buttons, bows and bits of wood on to your page. Again, there are many kinds available. Ask your craft shop for advice on the different kinds and strengths of glue you may need.

When using vellum paper, you will need a special 'invisible' glue but transparent photo splits are probably a better option. Photo splits also work well for sticking down ribbon.

Lastly you'll need foam adhesive. This is specially manufactured for scrapbooking and there are various kinds available. First of all there are glue dots, which are very expensive for the amount you get and which can only be used for certain projects. There are also 3-D foam squares and strips, which are two adhesive sheets with a spongy layer in between. Simply peel off the protective layers on both sides and use as you would thick double-sided adhesive tape. 3-D squares are available in black and white in both large and small squares.

Foam squares are also obtainable in thick and thin strips. Squares and strips work equally well and in time you'll discover which kind you prefer to work with on your different projects.

There are many different kinds of glue available

ALBUMS

You don't need to buy an album immediately, although you'll certainly need one later. Albums are expensive and only imported ones are available. However, classes are often offered where you can learn to make your own. Albums are made for two paper sizes (see Paper, page 6). The screws used to hold the album together may be substituted by a longer screw and so make it possible for more pages to be added. These screws are usually available at hardware stores.

As soon as you've made your first few scrapbooking pages, you'll want to buy an album. Make sure that you really like the album and that it will suit your requirements before purchasing it.

Album pockets and screws

ALBUM POCKETS

When you purchase an album, you'll also get album pockets to use inside the album. These pockets are made of polypropylene plastic and are acid free. Your completed scrapbook page is placed into the pocket, firstly to protect it and secondly to store it in your album. These pockets can be purchased individually or in packets of six. There are many kinds of pockets available, the only difference between them being the positioning and number of holes.

Albums are expensive, so make sure you really like the one you purchase and that it suits your requirements

It doesn't really matter if you buy the wrong size, as you may simply punch holes where needed to fit into your album. The fact that you can buy screws of different lengths helps to keep your album reasonably full, thereby allowing the pockets to weigh down on each other, and prevent the holes from tearing.

PENS AND PENCILS

Once again, use only acid-free products. All gel pens are acid free and there are also certain thicker ones that are acid free. Simply read the information on the pen itself. All grey pencils and also aquarelle-type pencils for colouring in may be used, as they are all acid free. Certain glitter pens are acid free and there are also acid-free paints available. Always be sure to read the label to make quite certain.

Acid-free chalk is also obtainable in various coloured blocks. Simply apply the product with your finger or an ear bud. Because chalk is expensive, it's a good idea to make sure you like the chalked effect before acquiring a whole set.

Use only acid-free pens and pencils

Acid-free chalk is obtainable in coloured blocks and can be applied with an ear bud

LIGHT BOX OR PHOTO PENCILS

A light box is used to mark the back of a photo to indicate where you want to cut it. It's convenient working with a light box, but it is not at all essential. If you don't have a light box, though, simply hold the photo against a window where the light shines through brightly.

A much cheaper and more convenient option is using a photo pencil. Photo pencils are dark blue and waxy. You can use them to draw on the front of a photo without damaging it. Once you've cut out the photo, place it on a piece of scrap paper and simply wipe away the pencil marks with a tissue. The reason for using scrap paper is because the wax cannot be erased from ordinary paper.

A light box and photo pencil

CROPPING EQUIPMENT

A whole variety of cropping equipment is used in scrapbooking. The most common tool is certainly an ordinary pair of paper scissors. Obtain both a large and small pair of pointed scissors. There are also assorted pinking shears available and it would be a good idea to acquire a selection. Some pinking shears have interchangeable blades – one set of shears with three or four different kinds of pinking blades.

A craft knife is also very important, particularly when you have to cut out inner frames. Always make sure that the blade is sharp and do your cropping on a cutting (self-healing PVC) mat. For me, a large perspex board does the trick for both cropping and pasting.

A guillotine is a very accurate cropping instrument for scrapbooking. They are available in several sizes, but rather spend a bit more and make sure that 12 x 12 inch (30.48 x 30.48 cm) paper fits into it. The advantage of using a guillotine is that you can cut straight lines quickly and easily without first having to measure them. A very important principle to keep in mind when using a guillotine is that the straight edge of your paper must be against the side of the cutting edge, and that you should then cut towards that side. It makes no difference whether you hold the guillotine in such a way that you cut towards you or away from you, the only important thing is to cut towards the side that is held against the edge. The reason for this is that if the paper is not pressed against the edge when you draw the blade over it, it could come out skew.

A variety of scissors, pinking shears and other cropping equipment

EMBELLISHMENTS

To make a page even more interesting, any kind of embellishment can be used in scrapbooking. Most of the decorations available in craft shops are acid free, but if in any doubt, don't paste them directly on to the photo itself.

If, for example, you want to paste something like an airline ticket on the page, you could make a little sleeve to hold it or mat your photos on acid-free paper in order to create a division between the photos and the ticket.

Any wood is safe to use in scrapbooking. Bits of fabric, ribbon, cotton, felt and lace also look pretty. Serviettes and paper doilies are also acid-free. An easy rule to follow is that all natural materials are acid-free.

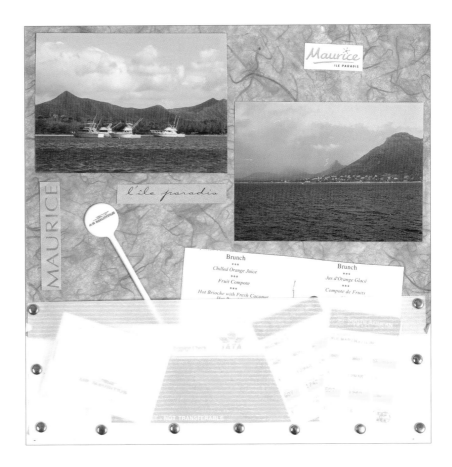

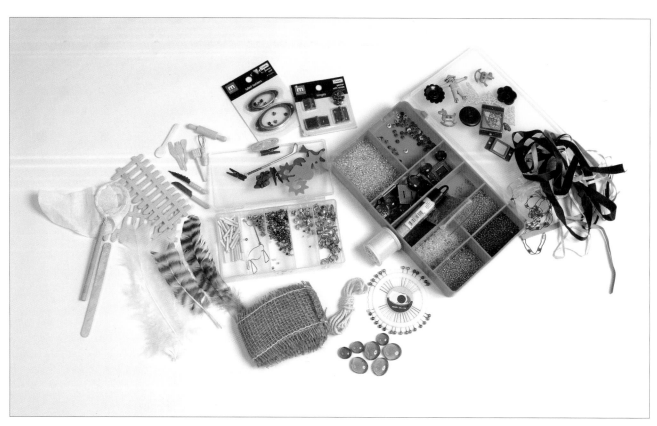

Interesting embellishments make scrapbooking colourful and fun

Examples of the many kinds of stickers available

STENCILS

Stencils are inexpensive, and you can easily make your own by cutting out patterns on old X-rays. Stencils are particularly useful if you are not very artistic or want to use the same design over and over again. Stencils that have simple shapes such as circles, ovals, hearts, squares and diamonds for cutting out photos, make the task mere child's play.

PHOTOGRAPHS

Last, but certainly not least, are the photographs. You could make pages that feature no photos at all and only have mementoes, such as entrance tickets, a map of a particular place or even pretty postcards, but generally the photos are the main reason for doing scrapbooking.

Don't worry about the quality of the photographs. Naturally you would prefer to have only beautiful, flawless photos, but unless you're an expert photographer, there is only a very slim chance that all your photos will be of excellent quality. As you progress with scrapbooking, you'll find it easier to simply crop those parts of the photos you don't want to include. You'll also discover that you'll develop a new eye for what to photograph and what your photos should look like. Read up on how to take better photos, but never throw your bad ones into the bottom of a box or ignore them when scrapbooking. You'd be surprised to see how lovely even the least attractive photos can look on the right scrapbook page.

If you are not very artistic, stencils will help you create many attractive letters and shapes

ADVANCED EQUIPMENT

There is an endless supply of equipment available for scrapbooking, but most of us can't afford to buy all of the tools. Find other scrapbooking enthusiasts and form a group to share equipment. In this way there'll be no need for each person to buy everything, and it would also be a good way of finding out what tools are used most and what you would like to acquire for yourself.

Here are just a few examples of the advanced equipment you may want to purchase:

EMBOSSING EQUIPMENT

Two embossing techniques are used in scrapbooking, namely wet embossing and dry embossing. For wet embossing you need stamps as well as an embossing stylus or inkpad. Embossing styli are available in different colours and there is even one with transparent ink. You also need embossing powder to go with the stylus, and this is available in various colours. The metallic colours are a firm favourite. This equipment is available at most craft shops and is reasonably priced.

For dry embossing you need a different kind of embossing stylus. It looks almost like a crochet hook, and you could indeed use a crochet hook for this purpose. Embossing styli are available in varying thicknesses.

Brass stencils can be used together with the stylus to simply trace the pattern of the stencil on to the paper. It's a little easier if you do it on a spongy surface. Take care, however, that the surface doesn't give too much, or you'll continually be making holes in the paper. There are also various embossing tables available. They work very well,

Equipment used for wet embossing

but are expensive. Various stencils are available that are specifically designed for the different tables on which embossing is done. Therefore you don't have to work on a soft surface, because in this instance you're working with two stencils, with the paper in the middle. In this way there is just enough space to transfer your pattern on to the paper successfully, without tearing the paper.

PUNCHIES

Punchies are pretty well known and available everywhere. They are useful in many art forms, especially card making where they are used regularly. There are three kinds of punchies: the most common ones punch out different shapes, for example circles, frogs and hearts. The second type is a corner punchie, which punches a 90° corner and works very well for decorating photo corners. The last kind is a line punchie, which imprints a pattern in a straight line. It is designed to either punch out a single pattern only, or punch out a continuous line and in this way create a border at the edge of your page or photo.

Punchies are very useful in scrapbooking

Dry embossing equipment

EYELETS AND RIVETS

An eyelet is a metal circle you press into paper or fabric to make a small hole. Rivets are similar to eyelets; however, they don't make holes, but look like the top of a thumbtack. The same eyelets and rivets used in needlework can be used in scrapbooking. They are attached with eyelet pliers. The disadvantage of working with this tool is that it can only be used approximately 2 cm from the edge of the paper. Special eyelets and rivets, much smaller in size and available in different colours and patterns, have been designed specifically for scrapbooking, but you would need to use special metal pens to attach them to the paper. One of these metal pens has a point in the shape of a sharp-rimmed circle that cuts the hole in your paper. The other has a sharp point, like a pencil, used to bend over the side of the eyelet or rivet. You'll also need to use a hammer in conjunction with these metal pens. The advantage of these tools is that they can be used on any part of the page.

PAPER CRIMPER

There are many different kinds, shapes and sizes of paper crimper available, but the most common is the apparatus that makes ordinary corrugated ribbing. Buy the biggest one you can afford, then you'll be able to turn larger pieces of paper to get a ribbed effect.

A paper crimper gives paper a ribbed effect

The tools used for pressing eyelets and rivets into paper or fabric

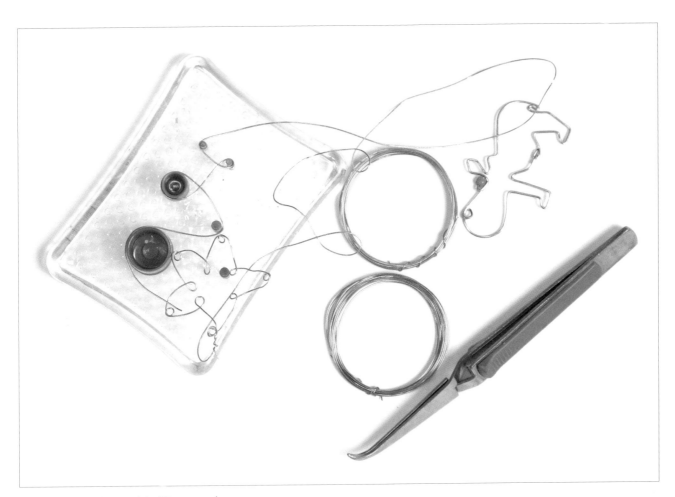

A Thing-A-Ma-Jig® used in filigree work

FILIGREE EQUIPMENT

Nowadays there are many tools on offer in craft shops with which to do filigree work with craft wire. Ordinary wire can also be used, but craft wire is much softer and easier to work with, and obtainable in a variety of colours. If you like filigree work, you'll need cutting-tongs and a pair of sharp-pointed pliers. There is also a tool called a Thing-A-Ma-Jig® that rolls wire up and straightens it out again. It can be found in craft shops.

NEEDLEWORK EQUIPMENT

If you want to use ribbon or thread on your page, you will definitely need a thick needle or a fine-pointed awl for making holes in the paper. Once the holes have been made, ribbon or cotton can be threaded through them. Transparent thread is also useful for attaching all sorts of embellishments, as well as wire, to a page without the thread being too noticeable.

Needlework equipment

Parchment art equipment

PARCHMENT ART EQUIPMENT

Parchment art is inkwork, embossing and piercing on thick vellum paper whereby delicate lace patterns are formed. It is really an art form in its own right, but works very well in making a special page in your album. However, you need parchment art equipment for such a project. If you're a whiz at scrapbooking, it will be worth your while to purchase this equipment, since it can also be used for other art forms, such as card making.

The minimum requirements for parchment art are a perforating tool (single needle), a round-tipped embossing stylus, white parchment ink and a sharp-tipped ink pen (you could also use a white gel pen), a soft but firm pressure pad and lastly, you may consider buying the wax which helps the embossing pen glide easily and smoothly over the paper. Of course, you will also need natural parchment paper. Parchment paper is like vellum paper, only a lot thicker.

QUILLING EQUIPMENT

Quilling is the art of winding paper strips into spools. Like parchment art, quilling is also an art form in its own right, and many card makers are familiar with it. One basically needs thin strips of paper as well as a special pen, which has two metal bits that the paper is hooked onto. By turning the pen, the paper is wound around the metal to make a paper spool used for creating different pictures.

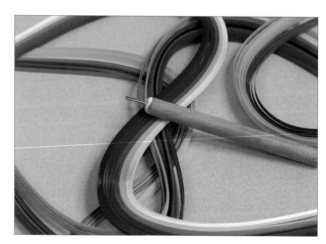

TWO IMPORTANT TERMS

CROPPING

There are a variety of reasons why you would crop photos. The most common reason is to cut them into specific shapes to suit your page. For instance, crop a birthday photo into the shape of a cake, a photo of washing into the shape of a shirt, or a fishing photo into a fish shape. A stencil is usually used for this, but it could also be cut free hand. The easiest way to do this, particularly if you don't have a light box, is to use a photo pencil.

PLEASE NOTE
On the example pages throughout the book, the word *Journalling* has been inserted in the spaces where journalling can be added.

Remember that photo pencil marks cannot be erased from ordinary paper. Once you've cropped your photo, place it on a piece of scrap paper, and wipe it with a tissue. Also wipe the stencil or ruler, or it will leave a mark the next time you use it on paper.

A second reason for cropping photos is to remove unnecessary background in the photo. In this way you create a focal point by removing the busy background. Once again, you could crop it into a shape, as shown here, or simply minimise the photo.

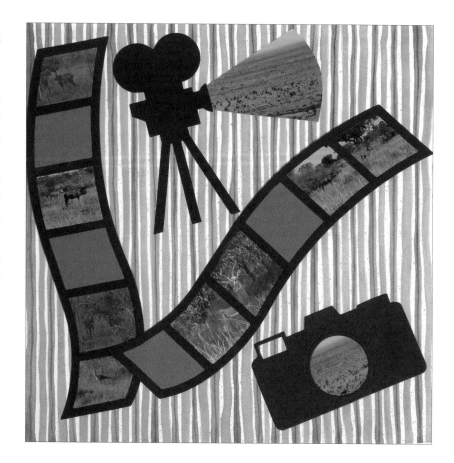

A photo can also be silhouetted by cutting along the profile or outlines of the person or object in the photo. A partial silhouette can be acquired by, for example, cutting the outline of the top part of the person and leaving the rest of the photo intact.

Never feel obliged to crop all the photos on a page to the same size or shape. Play around with different forms.

There are various artistic techniques for which cropping can be used that will be dealt with later in the book. A few examples are mosaic work, weaving and links. In all of these, the photo is cropped and then attached to the paper in a certain way.

Cropping not only makes it possible to improve bad photos, but also to remove blunders, people or undesirable objects from the photos, or to be able to fit in more photos on to a scrapbook page. There are times, however, when you shouldn't crop. Here are a few examples:

When working with heritage photos (you may have only one print of a certain person or event and no negative), it is sometimes better to make a colour copy of the photo and to work with the copy. Even when copying black-and-white photos, they should preferably be colour copied. The quality is just so much better. If there are historical items or places in the photo, it's best not to crop them at all – your descendants will appreciate being able to see these things in the photo.

Polaroid® photos should also not be cropped because there are chemical substances between the photo layers which, as soon as they are cropped, undergo a change that causes the photo to lose its colour.

If you have a photo that is a real work of art, it's better not to cut it. The same applies to photos taken in a studio. Always remember that a photo is cropped to ultimately improve it and when you tamper with a work of art you seldom improve the end product.

Example of a Polaroid® photo, which should not be cropped

MATTING (ALSO KNOWN AS MOUNTING)

When a photo is matted, it is pasted on to paper, which is cut slightly larger than the photo and so forms a frame around it. The most common way of matting is simply to crop a photo (if that's what you want to do), measure it, calculate the size of the frame and then cut out the bigger shape from the paper on which the photo will be pasted.

Of course, it's not always necessary to mat photos.

Matting can also be made more decorative by cutting the frame with pinking shears.

Give a photo more dimension by matting it more than once.

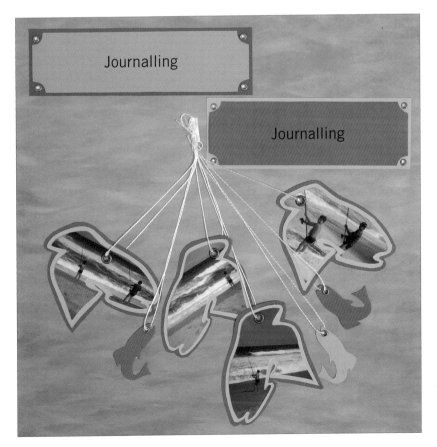

A photo can be matted four times or even more. It's a good idea to use the space between two layers on which to write your caption or title.

Mats don't necessarily all have to be the same shape.

Matting need not have the same shape as the photo.

Matting can be varied by cutting one layer with an ordinary pair of scissors and the next one with pinking shears. You could also apply embellishments to the mats.

Matting combined with a photo can create a totally new picture.

Use a punchie to make a mat more decorative.

Matting can cover up a large part of the page, thus forming a new background page.

Use matting as the basis on which to apply embellishments.

Matting itself can be the embellishment.

The title or journalling can be matted in a square. In this example the photo is not matted at all, but the embellishments form a frame around part of the photo.

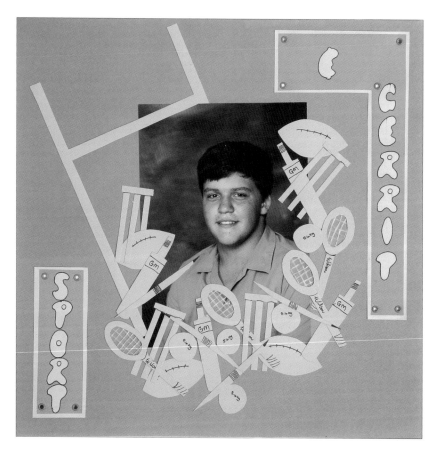

Contrasting colours can be used when matting a photo.

Letters can also be matted.

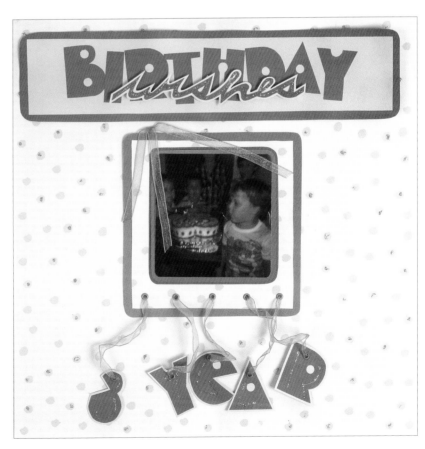

Matting certainly makes your scrapbook page interesting and helps with the repetition of certain shapes or colours. It creates a flow and allows the eye to be guided over the page, making it enjoyable for the person viewing your scrapbook pages.

BASIC PRINCIPLES

HOW TO SELECT PAPER FOR A SCRAPBOOK PAGE

Since paper is the most important material one works with, besides the photos, it's essential to choose the right paper to complement your photos. There are various ways of choosing paper. Simply decide what looks attractive and what doesn't by placing photos on different sheets of paper. You'll often be amazed to see which multicoloured sheets match one another, or which plain colours go with the multicoloured ones. Try different combinations and choose the one that looks best. Here are a few principles to guide you in your choice of paper:

Paper depicting water can be used for swimming photos

1. Adapt the paper to the theme of your photos

This method works well when choosing patterned paper as a background for your photos. Select paper with an animal skin print, for example, for photos of a particular animal, such as a crocodile, leopard or zebra. Paper that depicts water can be used for swimming pool photos and patterned paper with a sea and palm tree theme for your island photos.

Paper depicting sun, sea and palm trees works well with island photos

2. Adapt the paper to the clothes and colours in photos

You'd be surprised how often you find paper that reminds you of a specific outfit. Red gingham paper goes well with a photo of someone with a red-checked dress.

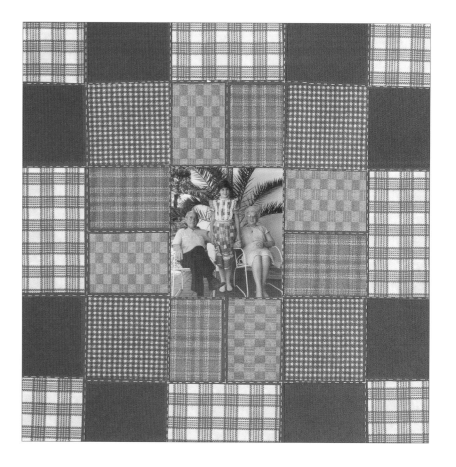

Put more life into black-and-white photos by choosing paper that reflects someone's original outfit. In this way, for instance, I imitated my mother's dress by using pink paper and pasting flowers along the edge that resemble the flowers on her dress.

Journalling

3. Adapt the paper to the occasion

Certain colours are often associated with particular occasions. Red and green, for example, are reminiscent of Christmas. A variety of printed paper has also been designed specifically for certain occasions.

Journalling

4. Adapt the paper to the theme of the page

One often has photos with no particular theme. Create a new theme by means of your caption, journalling or embellishments. You could, for instance, use red hearts for a page about a loved one, or apples for a page about the apple of your eye. In this example I used red apples as my theme and chose my colours accordingly. Note the cropping and matting to single out a certain person in a group photo.

Journalling

BASIC PRINCIPLES WHEN PLANNING A PAGE

I am totally convinced that there is no right or wrong way in scrapbooking. If the layout, colour, paper and shape work for you, then that's fine. In the long run, that's what scrapbooking is all about – portraying your personality in the pages of your scrapbook. In the course of time everyone develops their own style. However, when you need inspiration or, if for some reason, you're not happy with your page, here are a few basic guidelines.

1. Focal point

Most of your scrapbook pages should have a focal point that immediately draws your attention. Many scrapbooking experts say that this should in fact be a photo. I don't quite agree. Although the photos are definitely the most important item on the page, the focus could just as well be an embellishment or a caption. Everyone agrees, though, that there should be a focal point, and that the layout should guide your eye from that point. The focal point can be either photos or embellishments, and can be on any part of the page. Usually the middle of the page will be the focal point, but there are always exceptions. When, for some reason, your page just doesn't look right, in most cases the problem can be remedied by moving the focal point to the middle of the page.

2. Overlapping or not?

Overlapping is a technique that enables you to fit all your required objects on to a page. It can change a very rigid page into a flowing symphony of colour, shapes and photos. When creating more definite lines, however, you would seldom overlap your photos and plot everything on your page in straight lines instead.

3. Vary shapes and sizes

Various shapes and sizes ensure that your page remains interesting. It also helps when trying to fit more photos on to a page. Remember that it's not only the photos that may differ in shape and size, but also the embellishments.

4. More or enough?

How do you know when there's enough on a page, or when there should be something added? Do the pages look too bare or too full? These are difficult questions to answer. In most cases you'll have to decide this for yourself, since it all forms part of developing your own scrapbooking style. As a guideline, consider the theme, technique or general feeling you want to convey. This will vary from page to page. What I often do is put more photos or embellishments on to the page to see what it looks like, or I simply remove everything and very selectively choose a few items to put back. Sometimes it helps to just get up and walk around a bit, to rest your eyes and focus on something else. When you then return to the page, you immediately see whether it's alright and, if not, what the problem is.

HOW TO PUT TOGETHER YOUR FIRST SCRAPBOOK PAGE

Now that you have all the basic information about scrapbooking at your fingertips, your hands are probably itching to get to the actual cut-and-paste part. It's useful to get into a routine when making a scrapbooking page. Here are a few guidelines:

1. Choose all the photos you're going to need for the page

If you have many photos of the same occasion, spread them all out in front of you, and try to sort them into meaningful groups. The number of photos a page can accommodate varies from technique to technique, as well as from page to page. If you're making an ordinary page, between three and six photos will usually be sufficient, depending on how much the photos are cropped and matted.

2. Choose the different kinds of paper you wish to use

Re-read the guidelines on page 6 on how to select your paper. Usually a minimum of two kinds of paper is used per page. These could be two patterned, two plain or a patterned and a plain kind. However, there's nothing to stop you from choosing more than two.

3. Allow your photos and paper to lead you in deciding on a theme for your page

A cake, for instance, is often a special focal point at a children's party and therefore makes a fine theme for a scrapbooking page. If you're working with photos of a group of teenagers in a swimming pool, a good theme for the page would be wavelets, splashes of water and any other embellishments that suggest fun in the water. Waves also work well with sea holiday photos, or try a sandcastle, beach umbrella or large beach ball as the focal point for your page. At this stage it's important to begin forming an idea about what you want your page to look like. It needn't be planned in detail, as you'll naturally plan and make changes as the work on the page progresses.

4. Crop your photos

Refer to the guidelines on pages 19–21 about when to crop and when to use an entire photo. Keep the theme of your page in mind when deciding what shape to crop your photos. Crop them into starfish shapes for sea photos, water splashes for swimming pool photos or into circles, ovals or smaller rectangles. You could also silhouette your photos. Remember that they needn't all be the same shape or size.

5. Mat your photos

Refer to the ideas about matting (mounting) on pages 22–29 and decide whether or not to use more than one mat. Also decide how your mat should be cut – with pinking shears, an ordinary pair of scissors or by tearing. One golden rule is that if your background paper is patterned, it's better to mat on plain paper – but this is only a guideline and there are always exceptions. Put your photo on the paper you want to mat it on and then place this on the background paper to see whether the colours work. Certain colours will make your photos stand out more than others.

6. Now arrange your photos on the background paper, but don't paste them yet

Move the photos around on the page until you feel satisfied with their placement and the number of photos you have selected.

7. Decide on the embellishments you want to use on the page according to the theme

This could be anything from ribbon or bows, filigree work, tearing, chalking, punchies, buttons or any other embellishments you like.

8. Arrange the embellishments on your page together with the photos

Move them around if the picture doesn't look quite right, and remove some or add more. Remember to leave room for your captions and journalling.

9. Now work on your caption and journalling

Choose a particular spot on the page for your journalling, and remember to leave it open. Select a type of script for your caption and if you're going to cut out the letters, now is the time to do so. See the sections on creative captions (pages 44–50) and journalling (pages 50–51) before proceeding.

10. When the page looks right, start pasting

Use photo splits to attach photos and any large, flat embellishments. Use a glue stick for smaller bits of paper and ornamentation. Any raised decorations or decorations not made of paper should be pasted down with wet glue. Ribbons, wire and fabric can be sewn on with transparent thread, or you could test which glue sticks them down best. Ribbon can also be attached successfully with the transparent photo splits used for vellum paper.

11. If there is more journalling to be done, this should be done now

Remember that you want to tell a story about the photos, the occasion and the people. This will help you to decide what to write.

12. Once you're satisfied with your page and you've made all the final changes, insert the page into the protective album pocket

You'll be amazed at the difference it makes to the appearance of your page. Remember: there is no right or wrong way in scrapbooking. All that is required is for you to feel satisfied with the way your page looks and the story it tells.

BASIC IDEAS FOR PAGE LAYOUTS

It's important to bear in mind that every page in your album does not necessarily have to display a different technique. You can simply follow the guidelines above for the layout of most of the pages.

To prevent you from getting stuck in one particular style, however, it's advisable that you try as many different layouts as possible. The fact that you will be choosing a different theme for each page also helps to make the pages interesting, since you'll be using different embellishments on each page.

For starters the following pages provide a few basic ideas for arranging your pages, followed by a few more specific ideas on page layout. Remember that this list is not in any way complete, since every page layout creates a different look.

1. Divide your page into quarters

Use two paper colours for the background and cut them into quarters. Paste the quarters alternately opposite each other on to the page.

2. Work with strips

Cut your paper into thinner strips or use small sheets of paper. Vertical strips are used in the example below to create a picture.

3. Work with squares

Squares can be used in different ways. Here are a few ideas: paste three or four squares in a row and use this as a background for your caption or on which to stick embellishments, in this case flowers. A row of squares can be pasted down the side or along the bottom of the page.

Paste small squares all around the edge of the page to form a frame (see example on the right). Once again they can be used for journalling or embellishments, or can be cut from different kinds of paper and used alternately.

Another idea would be to cut out three large squares and place them on the page diagonally to change the background paper. Use same-sized squares of paper and photos, and paste them in alternate rows for an eye-catching effect.

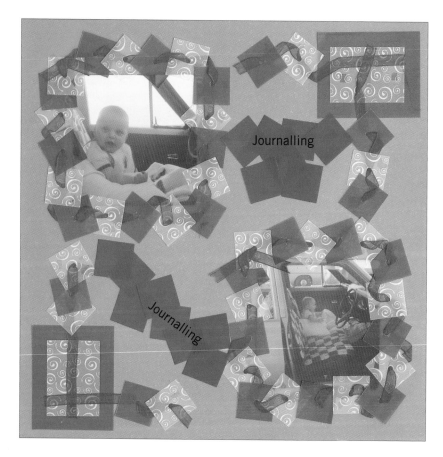

4. Work with triangles

Triangles are very useful on a square page. Once again, you could divide your page into quarters, and then divide each quarter into two triangles. Cut squares in half diagonally to form triangles and arrange them in various ways on your background page.

5. Create a new picture

Since so many photos have a definite theme according to which the page can be designed, it's often best to lay out your page by creating a new picture. Simply cut out all your pictures according to the theme, and create a new picture by using your photos and embellishments.

DIAGRAMMATIC IDEAS FOR PAGE LAYOUTS

Use these ideas for specific layouts when you are at a loss as to what to do with your photos. Simply choose a layout you like (see the templates below) and adapt it to your own paper and photos. I have made two examples of each layout. They are depicted below (template A) and on the opposite page (template B).

Compare the example pages above. The left-hand page shows that embellishments don't necessarily have to be items stuck on to the page as in the case of the example page on the right. You can simply use torn paper in such a way that it can be pasted in layers on to the background page or used as mats for photos. You can even tear holes in paper and use these as frames for photos.

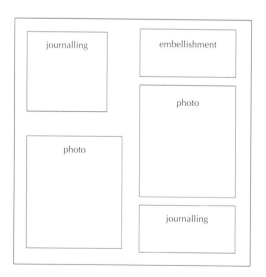 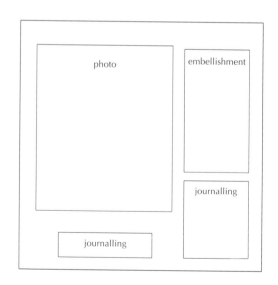

Template A

Template B

Scrapbooking pages following the layout in template B

CONCLUSION

When you feel that you have mastered your equipment and the basic principles of scrapbooking, start learning different techniques and apply them. In the next few pages a number of general techniques will be explained and demonstrated by means of a number of examples. However, there are still many other scrapbooking techniques for you to learn, and nothing should prevent you from creating your own. Remember that you'll probably want to scrap many more photos, so you'll need lots of ideas. Sooner or later we all get stuck in a certain style and can think of nothing new. At times like these it's a good idea to go back to basics. Also look at the albums of as many other scrappers as possible, and purchase a few scrapbooking magazines. Make notes on the pages you like and in this way start your own library of ideas to which you can refer when inspiration fails. Enjoy your scrapbooking!

INTERESTING IDEAS

By now you should have a basic knowledge of scrapbooking – what it is, all the requirements and how to make a simple scrapbooking page. Let's now take a look at the journalling on your pages.

Because a scrapbook tells the story of your life, journalling on the pages is very important. It's generally here where many scrapbookers miss the mark, but it's definitely not something to become apprehensive about. You needn't use big words and perfect grammatical sentences; on the contrary, it's much better to write the way you speak. This is when your own personality should shine through, and not that of *The Oxford Dictionary*! Consider it an opportunity to record your thoughts and emotions, significant happenings and other information. In this section a few journalling ideas will be provided.

There are also ideas for making the pages of your album more attractive and interesting. You'll still need to apply all the basic guidelines for making a scrapbooking page, but there will be many new skills to learn. Among other things, we'll be looking at how to tear paper, how to crop photos, how to work with chalk, and how to use materials such as sewing thread, wire and cord on your pages.

CREATIVE CAPTIONS

When planning a caption, don't think of it as something that must necessarily be written by hand, but as a work of art that needs to be sketched and developed. Most of the time, a shorter caption is best, because often space is a factor, but this doesn't mean that a long caption is taboo. Here are a few ideas to make your captions eye-catching and creative:

DRAW, DON'T WRITE

First do a trial run by drawing the letters you're going to use on a bit of scrap paper. Next, lightly draw the letters in pencil onto the scrapbook paper, then go over them with gel pens. If you're using a light-coloured pen, rub out a small section of the pencilled letter at a time, and then immediately re-draw that bit with the pen. Continue until the whole letter has been completed. In this way, you won't lose all your lines and the pencil lines won't shine through.

SPACING

If your letters don't touch or overlap, make sure that the spaces between the letters are equal.

SLANT

If your letters slope to the left or right, ensure that they all slant at the same angle, or they could look very untidy. As always, there are exceptions to every rule. If you want the caption to look as though it was written by a grade-one child, for example, you may want to play with the slant.

THEME

Use the theme of your page to adapt the letters accordingly. For example, for photos of the Anaconda roller coaster taken at Gold Reef City, adapt the letters to look like snakes.

Here the captions were made to look like a roller coaster, as well as reflect the theme of the Anaconda snake

ADD SOMETHING SMALL

Use an ordinary letter stencil and modify the letters with something small so that they take on a whole new look. For instance, add little bits of grass and flowers to the base of the letters. You could also cut out the letters and stick beads on to them. Or why not cut out letters from double-sided adhesive tape and sprinkle them with beads?

CHANGE YOUR SCRIPT

Write with a calligraphy pen and make the letters a little longer with narrower horizontal lines.

Add a small dot to the end of each line, or draw short lines through the shaft of each letter. Adding a swirl at the end of a line changes a letter's appearance dramatically.

CHANGE THE VERTICAL SHAFT OF THE LETTERS

This creative lettering is an easy way to give a fresh look to a stencil letter. The vertical shaft can be changed into a number of objects. Draw a palm tree, for example, if you have photos of the sea or an island. Or change the shaft to a baby's bottle on a page with baby photos. Any embellishment can be used to change the vertical shaft. Another example is to paint toothpicks to look like porcupine quills. I also came across a miniature wooden coat hanger and used it for the horizontal line of the letter T.

THE INTERIOR

You could modify a thick stencil letter to go with your page. Draw pizza slices in the letters to go with photos of a pizza party (right). You could also draw a picture or write something in white on a dark green or black background to resemble work on a blackboard to go with school photos.

THE EXTERIOR

The exterior of a letter can also be embellished. For instance, draw an Easter egg and then a letter on the inside of the egg. Do the same with Christmas decorations. You could also use store-bought embellishments as an exterior for letters, for example glass pebbles. Pasting them on top of each letter makes the letters look bigger. Brightly coloured slides can be used as a frame around letters.

COLOURING IN

The insides of letters can simply be coloured in with crayons or aquarelle pencils.

FILL THE SPACES

The open spaces in some letters such as the A, B, D, g and so on, can quite easily be transformed into something interesting. On a page about outdoor life, for example, you can draw little insects in these spaces. Punchies or plastic embellishments, such as a bone for a page with dog photos, can be pasted in the spaces. Eyelets and rivets can also be used.

EXTRA ORNAMENTATION

Letters need not only be embellished with drawing. Go a step further and use embellishments in conjunction with letters. The possibilities are endless. You could, for instance, make tags and decorate them with a letter on each. Or use different kinds and colours of cord or ribbon to decorate the letters individually or as a whole. Curl wire around a pen, thread beads on to it and drape it around your letters.

Buy small embellishments like miniature scissors, pens and pencils at your craft shop and paste them in the vicinity of your caption. For a page with baby pictures, you could cut up a doily and paste it on a pink or blue background, then cut out pink or blue letters from paper and paste these on top. Complete the picture by fastening small nappy pins on to the paper.

Another option is to cut squares from plain paper and cut letters from patterned paper. Paste the letters on top of the squares and attach the individual squares to the page with coloured pins or miniature clothes pegs. Sew little buttons on to your page or paste them in a pattern that follows the line of the letters.

Tearing can also be used to make your letters more attractive and give them more than one colour. Paste torn brown paper on to a sheet of blue paper. Draw stencilled or hand-written letters over the pasted part. Cut them out and use them on your page. The two-colour letters resemble the sea breaking on the shore (the letters PQR at the bottom right in this example have been done in this way).

Hopefully the above ideas will give your imagination free rein. So much can be done with the caption of a page. It's not always necessary to use complicated techniques to make your albums unique. After cropping your photos neatly, matting them and pasting them on beautiful paper, all that's left to do to make your page look even more like a work of art is to decorate the caption in an eye-catching way.

JOURNALLING

By doing scrapbooking you're preserving your photos and memories for your descendants. That's the real reason for working with acid-free products – to prevent your photos from deteriorating during the course of time. With the help of your photos you want to tell a story. So, apart from the photos, journalling is the most important component of your album.

However, it can be a problem deciding what you should write. Here are a few easy tips to follow when you simply can't think of what to put down on paper:

W, W, W, W, H and W?

Ask yourself the following questions: Who, What, Where, When, How and Why? This is an important starting point when you set about doing journalling.

EMOTIONS

How did you feel when a photo was taken? In the case of a picture of a father and his first-born son, journalling would do well to focus on the proud feeling the father has for his son, more than on the precise date (when), place (where), and so on. Remember that it's not a case of simply reproducing a calendar of every single thing you've done in your life, but also of describing how you felt. Depict your own life and that of your family, and don't forget to reflect each one's personality.

THE STORY OF THE PHOTO

Don't be too repetitive – this will water down the relevant information. If, for instance, the photo clearly reflects a birthday boy or girl blowing out four candles, you needn't repeat that in your caption; incorporate it instead, e.g. 'He blew out all four candles with one blow!' Keep in mind that a photo tells its own story, and that you just need to fill in the gaps.

Take photos with the specific purpose of complementing your journalling. For instance, a photo of a welcome sign at the entrance to a town can serve as a caption. In this way your journalling is made more interesting.

FREEHAND OR STENCILLING/PRINTING?

There will undoubtedly be times when you'll want to do your journalling on a computer. There will also be times when you'll want a page to look formal and a stencil will be used for the journalling. Remember, however, that your own handwriting is best. Your descendants will attach much more sentimental value to hand-written memories than to a typed version – even if you think your handwriting is unattractive. Don't be afraid of the actual writing or of perhaps making mistakes. You'll naturally want your pages to look professional, but a little mistake here and there will reflect the human element and be greatly treasured by your descendants.

HOW MANY WORDS?

The length of the journalling does not matter at all. Just remember to tell the story.

MAKE A CONNECTION

Make a connection between a photo and something else. It could be an interesting tale about how you got your first bike depicted by a photo of your children on their bikes. It could even be information about the lifestyle of your ancestors who didn't have a fridge, displaying a photo of your brand new fridge. In other words, the journalling you place with your photos need not necessarily reflect that specific photo.

GENERAL INFORMATION

If, for example, you have a photo of a glass blower you visited, it would be a good idea to provide more details about the art of glass blowing than to expand on the occasion itself. For a visit-to-the-zoo theme, jot down snippets of information on each animal. In this way general information is provided about the subject of the photo.

RHYMES AND VERSES

Sometimes it's a good idea to use quotations. Nursery rhymes come in handy for the hundreds of photos mothers usually take of their offspring. Use the words of songs or poems that appropriately reflect an emotion or situation. However, don't fall into the habit of never writing down your own thoughts.

INFORMAL LANGUAGE

Don't try to use the longest words in the dictionary. Your scrapbooking album is not a linguistic project – it's a reflection of your life and personality. Write the way you speak – in this way your descendants will learn a lot more about you.

KEEP IT INTERESTING

Tell a story. Writing: 'The cake had all been polished off, plates and glasses lay about everywhere, the music didn't let up until three – we really celebrated my 40th birthday with a bang!' sounds more exciting and describes the atmosphere of the event much more effectively than: 'My 40th birthday party was very nice.'

SAYINGS

When you really want to capture the personality of each of your friends and family in your album, write down a saying that that specific person is known for. Just make sure you have it exactly right before you put the words down on paper.

DETAIL

It's important to provide as much detail as possible, particularly when describing an occasion or situation. Detail will give credibility to your storytelling and also hold the reader's attention. Include detail in such a way that it is not repetitive, yet includes all the most important aspects of the occasion.

FIRST PERSON OR NOT?

It's a personal choice whether to refer to 'I' and 'we' when journalling or to refer to yourself in the third person. It's important to remember that a few generations from now people will perhaps not know who the 'I' and 'we' in the photos are.

TEARING AND CHALKING

These are very popular techniques to use in scrapbooking. They're inexpensive, easy to do and can turn an ordinary page into a feast for the eye.

Plain paper tears very well, because it leaves an interesting white edge where the paper has been torn (see right). Any paper can be torn – even handmade or vellum paper.

Torn paper has a rough and a smooth side. Either side can be used on the front, but the rough side usually has the more interesting texture and can be coloured with chalk more easily. An easy way to tear the paper so that the rough side is on the front is to hold the part of the paper you want to use in your left hand with the front facing you, and then tearing it towards you with your right hand. In this way the rough part of the tearing will be on the front of the paper.

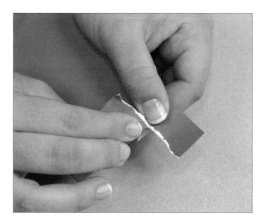

Hold the part of the paper you want to use in your left hand and tear towards you with your right hand

Vellum paper tears very well

Tearing can make a page very appealing, particularly if you create a background with only torn pieces of paper on it.

If you want to tear handmade paper, particularly if it has a complicated shape, it's better to dampen it slightly along the tear line. Take a side in each hand and pull the paper apart, rather than performing a tearing action.

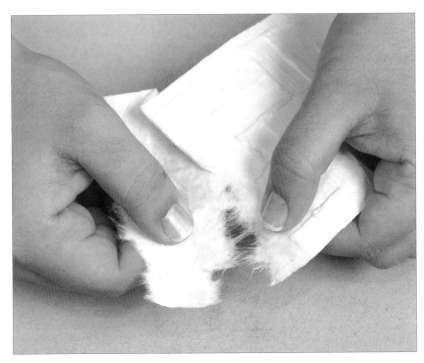

Tearing can be used to form a frame around your page.

Feel free to tear shapes from paper. In the example below, I tore uneven circles, crumpled the paper, smoothed it out again and rounded it off with chalking. A few of these circles were pasted on top of one another to form a rose used in the name at the bottom. I also tore hearts, which were used as frames. Make the decorations to suit the page.

The Serendipity technique works very well in tearing. This is an easy technique where different kinds of paper are torn into small pieces. Choose plain and patterned paper as well as paper that has different textures, and tear them all into small pieces (about 1–2 cm). Paste the pieces randomly on a piece of paper of your choice (white paper works well) using a glue stick. Don't follow a set pattern when pasting the scraps. Cut patterns or the letters for your caption from this paper, and use them to decorate your page. However, don't cut the shape from the white paper first and then paste the bits on to it. Always paste a larger area with scraps first and then cut out the shapes.

Chalking and tearing complement each other very well. Chalking is simply colouring in the torn paper with different chalk colours, thereby creating an even more colourful and interesting effect. Use a contrasting or slightly darker colour and apply it to the rough part of the torn paper. In this way the tearing is accentuated. Chalk can be applied with your finger, cotton wool or an ear bud. Chalking can also be used to create a new picture on a white page. Feel free to use stencils to help you with this.

Chalking works well in making captions more interesting or creating the illusion of water. For this double-page spread I bought the predesigned paper on the left. The caption on the paper lay towards the right-hand side of the page, which created the impression that it formed part of a double-page spread. However, I couldn't find a matching right-hand page, so I simply took chalk in hand and made the page on the right myself. Don't feel obliged to buy predesigned paper. Design your own page from scratch.

Use a combination of chalk and pencils. With pencils more detail can be drawn and with chalk a larger surface can be coloured in more easily.

CREATIVE CROPPING

By means of creative cropping a large variety of stunning pages can be produced. Paper and photos can be cut in clever ways and the cutouts pasted creatively on the page. Here are a few ideas to inspire you.

It's sometimes difficult to see a person or object in a photo. This often happens with wildlife photos, when a leopard or lion, for example, simply refuses to lie alongside the road in plain sight. An easy way to highlight the picture is to simply crop a part of your photo so that the frame or background paper can be seen behind it. This immediately focuses your attention on the most important part of the photo.

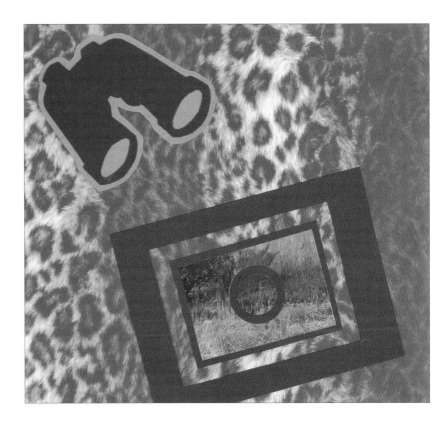

A variation of this technique is to crop the photo into several sizes of the same shape and then paste them in different ways on to the background paper.

Make a boring picture look more striking by cutting the photo into horizontal or vertical strips and then pasting them a little way apart. This is almost like regular mosaic (page 92) but is done in strips, not blocks. In this example, I framed the photos in black.

Take this technique further by cutting out the profile or outlines in the photo. In this example, I cut out the curves of the mountains and landscape and the two parts of the toilet. The photo can be pasted in one of two ways: the mountain and landscape can be cut into strips and pasted a little apart on the matting. Or if something in the middle is cut out, like the island in the photo, the dam or the toilet basin and cistern, you would first mat that part of the picture separately on the same colour paper used for matting the photo, and then paste it over the hole from which it was cut. In this way, an effect is achieved that the photo has been stretched.

It's also possible to crop only parts of a photo, top and bottom, or left and right, into thin strips and then paste them apart slightly to make it look as though the photo has been stretched. In this example I didn't re-paste it in a rectangle, but created steps for a more eye-catching effect. Photos can also be used to form a title or caption on the page.

Another clever way of stretching a photo is by cutting lines in it. Don't cut the lines right through though, so that the photo remains intact. Cut the lines near the edge of the photo so that it forms an even curve when you pull it apart. In this example, I cropped the photo with wavelet-scissors to imitate the water in the photo and background page. See the pattern template (wavy waters page 140) to cut the lines in this example, but it can of course be adapted in any other way to allow the curves to go in the other direction.

Try this clever technique to pep up a page. Cut any shape from paper. In this example I cut out the figure '8'. Paste your photos with temporary glue or attach them lightly with photo splits on to the shape. Turn the shape over and trace its outlines on to your photos. Dislodge the photos and cut them out along the lines. Your photos should now be cut into at least two parts (in this case into three parts). Paste the paper shape (the '8') on to your background page, then paste the photos in their exact positions over it. Those parts of the photos pasted on the outside of the shape need not be cropped any further – simply paste them a little distance from the shape. However, those pieces pasted on the inside should be cropped a bit smaller along the cutting line to be able to fit in. Paste them a little further from the shape.

Punchies make detailed cropping easy. In this example I used a corner punchie. Punch out the corners of a few squares of paper, then trim each one a lot smaller so that it forms a triangle, with the sharp point opposite to where the corner was punched (see below). Paste these punched shapes all around your photo to form a frame. Make an additional paper frame and paste it along the top of the punchies to finish them off neatly (see the example right).

Use creative cropping to make a frame for your photo with links that fold back and produce a lovely effect (see pattern template below). The half-moons are cut out with a craft knife, folded back and slotted in beneath the rounded part of the previous circle. The circular shape can be adapted to form an oval, square, oblong or any other shape. Half-moons can also be adapted to have sharp points or resemble wavelets.

Feel free to try new techniques and don't be afraid of cropping a photo (unless it's a heritage or Polaroid® photo). Should a photo be spoiled during cropping, simply use the negative to have a new one made.

SEWING THREAD AND OTHER ODDS AND ENDS

Sewing thread, ribbon, fabric, cord, wire and beads give your album page dimension and texture. If you're an avid needleworker, your other hobbies may easily be incorporated into scrapbooking. Cross-stitch, patchwork, ribbon embroidery and even filigree can be used quite successfully. You'd be surprised at how beautiful your pages can be made to look. Use the following techniques when working with these materials:

SEWING THREAD

Sew your photos together with sewing thread. First paste each photo on to the background page. Use a needle or a sharp-pointed awl to make holes where you would like to do the needlework, then simply use your needle and thread to sew through the holes and in this way produce a lovely effect. Plain paper on which journalling can be done may also be attached in this way.

Journalling

Journalling

This technique can be adapted slightly by using eyelets for the holes through which to run your thread. Cord, ribbon or wire can be used for this technique.

The thread need not always stitch photos or frames together neatly, but can be stretched across the page like a spider's web into which photos can be inserted and then pasted down.

Photos and embellishments needn't always be connected to one another. The photo, frame or decoration can simply be sewn on to your background page; but always remember to punch in the holes with a needle or sharp-pointed awl first. Work on a soft surface like a cutting mat or simply use a piece of polystyrene.

In this example, I sewed the blocks on to the background page. The paper blocks are therefore not pasted on to the page at all. Leave a small part of the block open and then stuff it with wadding before sewing it up. In this way I achieved a three-dimensional effect without using foam squares.

Thread beads on to sewing thread or wire and use this in your scrapbook. In this example, I threaded beads on to cotton strands and then attached them to the page with adhesive tape.

RIBBON

Ribbon can be used in many ways on your pages. Satin ribbon can be pasted with wet glue, but is inclined to leave a faint mark on the front. Use photo splits instead for satin and organza ribbon. I prefer to use transparent photo splits when working with ribbon because these are much thinner and smaller than ordinary photo splits. On this page (right), I made notches with a craft knife on the triangular pattern of the coloured mat paper and then simply threaded ribbon through them.

WIRE

Wind soft wire around a pencil to form a curl. Thread the wire in a zigzag pattern through eyelets and stick it on to the back of the page with adhesive tape. Thread some beads here and there to make the page more colourful. If you want to wind the wire around the caption, the letters will have to be reinforced. Mat the letters at least once or twice. In this example, I matted the letters a third time, but didn't cut the mat any bigger, so you can't see that it has been reinforced.

Using foam squares, paste the letters on to your background page. Now start on one side and make a hole in the background paper at the base of your first letter. Thread the wire through and stick it to the back of the background page with adhesive tape. Thread the wire around and through your letters as you like. At the last letter, make another hole and stick your wire on to the back of the page with adhesive tape. Some scrapbookers like to sew their wire on with transparent thread, but I find sticking it down simpler and easier.

Another way of curling wire is to use a paper crimper. It makes the wire look like corrugated iron. On this page (right), I threaded the wire through the journalling blocks using eyelets.

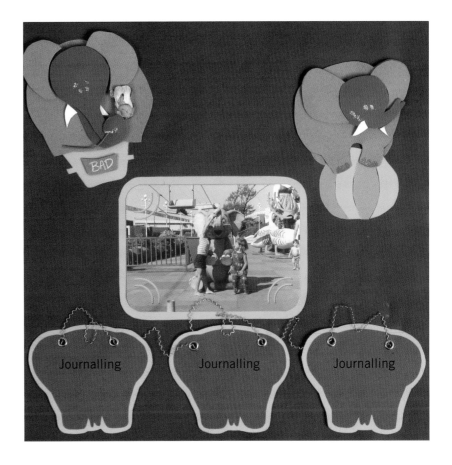

CORDING

Cording is a clever technique for scrapbooking. It's also a good substitute for projects that use ribbon and thread. In this example, I made a few knots in the cord (see page 140 for examples of knots you can use on your pages). Remember that you needn't complete a knot – stop halfway through and attach it as is (with wet glue or invisible thread). It then looks totally different. On this page I made four knots from a single kind of knot by stopping at the various stages of knotting before sticking the cord on to the page.

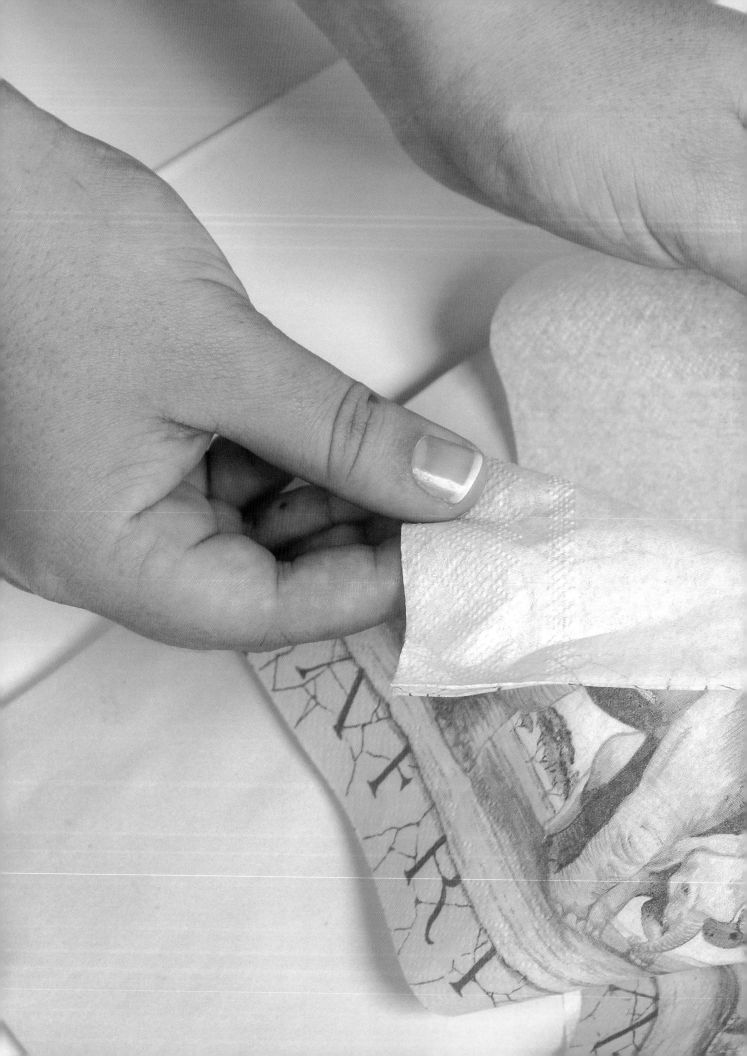

TECHNIQUES

In this chapter, both simple and advanced techniques are covered, for which you won't necessarily need very expensive equipment.

Some of the techniques, such as parchment art and quilling, are independent art forms that have entire books written about them. In the limited confines of this book, however, I cannot supply you with sufficient information to completely master these arts but, with the aid of the techniques explained here, you'll learn how to make really special scrapbook pages. If they appeal to you and you'd like to acquire more information about the individual art forms, I would suggest you get hold of books on each of them.

Scrapping with serviettes is a new scrapbooking technique that has thus far never been discussed in any book or magazine. I invented this technique myself when I discovered that serviettes are acid free. It's an easy technique to master without having to use any extra equipment. Another thing that counts in its favour is the fact that many different kinds of serviettes are available and they are relatively cheap.

In the requirements for each technique, I refer to the general requirements for undertaking that specific technique, and not to everything required for completing a particular example page. The reason for this is that scrapbooking is a personal art. Examples are there to inspire and shouldn't be copied exactly.

The basic scrapbooking tools I refer to in the requirements are tools such as glue, a pair of scissors, photos, paper, a ruler, pencils and so on needed to make a scrapbook page.

I hope you'll enjoy trying out these techniques.

LINKS

A Coluzzle® stencil set simplifies this technique quite a bit, as you get varying sizes of one shape on the Coluzzle® stencil. However, try the technique with an ordinary stencil that has one or two sizes of the same shape first. There are many of these stencils available in craft shops, and they are a great deal cheaper than buying the Coluzzle® mat, knife and stencil set. You will need three sizes of the same shape on the stencil you buy. In this project I have used a Coluzzle® set.

If you don't have a light box, you'll definitely need a photo pencil so that you won't draw a line over a face on a photo by mistake. A link page can be made of circles, squares or any other shape of your choice. In this example ovals were used.

REQUIREMENTS
- basic scrapbooking tools
- at least 4 or 5 photos
- background paper
- craft knife
- stencils
- photo pencil or light box

1 Place your smallest oval on the photo – it must cover the most important part of it. Using the photo pencil, draw the oval on your photo. Draw the next two sizes of the oval proportionally on the photo.

2 Using the craft knife, cut out the three ovals. You should have a complete oval and two oval frames. The smaller oval frame won't be used on this page, so you can either discard it or keep it for another page.

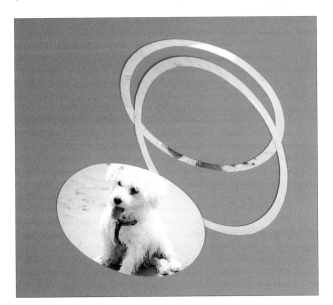

3 Repeat these two steps with all your photos.

4 Place the photos on to the page in such a way that the oval frames overlap one another. Using photo splits, stick the ovals on to the page. Where the frames overlap, slit open the bottommost frame so that it can be woven through the other oval frame like the links in a chain.

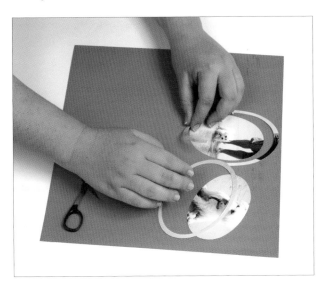

5 Using the glue stick, paste the ovals on to the page in such a way that they look as though they have been linked together. Make sure that the frame stuck on the top covers the slit in the bottom frame properly.

6 Complete the rest of the page with journalling and a caption.

DRY EMBOSSING

Embossing gives a page a three-dimensional effect. Pressure is applied to certain parts of the page causing them to be raised up. An embossing table with stencils and an embossing stylus are required to do embossing but, if you don't have an embossing table on which to press, use thicker stencils on an ordinary table top or craft mat. Place a few stencils on top of one another to acquire the right thickness. Craft shops sell special brass stencils that are thick enough, so you only need one stencil.

I use an embossing table like the one in the example on page 73. With an embossing table, stencils are sold in packets of two. The embossing table is designed in such a way that the two stencils fit onto each other and are kept in place by brackets, so they can't move around. The paper used for the embossing is held between the two stencils. You'll also need an embossing stylus, but a crochet hook or a dry Bic® pen also work well.

Any kind of paper is suitable for embossing, but very thin paper tears easily. The ordinary white paper that comes with album pockets is the ideal thickness. Vellum paper can also be used, but buy a thicker one that doesn't tear easily.

Frames, borders or pictures can be made with embossing. Don't be limited by your stencil. Create your own pictures – move the paper around beneath the stencil and use only parts of each stencil picture. Lengthen or shorten the pictures to form longer or shorter edges, or to form corners for a frame.

REQUIREMENTS
- basic scrapbooking tools
- embossing equipment
- paper for embossing

1 Crop and mat your photo any way you like. Place the photo on to the background paper and, using a pencil, mark the corners.

2 Select the picture you want to emboss from your assortment of stencils. Arrange the background paper in such a way that the picture fits properly into the frame space.

3 Use a thick embossing stylus to 'colour in' the shapes. Make even strokes so that the final product looks as though it has been pressed down and not drawn on.

4 When the picture has been embossed completely, use a thinner embossing stylus all around the border of the picture to make sure the end product looks finished off and that it protrudes well.

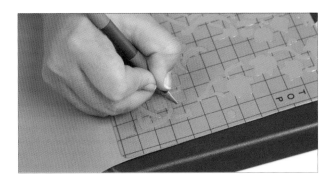

5 Now work all around the marked corners to form a complete frame.

6 Remember, the raised sections can be accentuated with chalking.

Complete the rest of the page by pasting the photo into the frame. Don't forget the journalling and caption.

WET EMBOSSING

For this project, powder and not pressure is used to do the embossing. Your pattern can be made with an ordinary stencil, but it's easy to do this project without a stencil. When working with an inkpad, however, you'll need a stamp.

An embossing stylus or embossing inkpad is always used with embossing powder. Both are available in a variety of colours, but the transparent ones are more commonly used and are a better investment.

In wet embossing, the paper is moistened with embossing ink so that the powder will stick to it. Ordinary coloured ink can also be used. A large variety of ink is available, but make sure that it's acid free. When working with ordinary ink, simply sprinkle transparent powder over it so that the colour of the ink shows through. Embossing ink works well for wet embossing because it takes longer to dry and thus gives you enough time to sprinkle over the powder and to melt it.

Store the powder in relatively large plastic containers that seal well. Put a plastic teaspoon in each one. In this way the powder can be poured out easily when needed and the unused powder returned to the container.

For wet embossing a heat source is required. I use an embossing heat tool, more commonly referred to as a heat gun, but if you don't have one, use a hairdrier, place your paper in a warm oven, or use any other heat source over which you have control. It's just important to have heat so that the powder sprinkled on to the paper is able to melt. When using a heat gun, the heat penetrates the powder from above; in the other methods the heat is applied from below.

A bag of anti-static powder is also very useful in wet embossing. These bags are hard to come by and quite expensive. A cheap alternative is to make your own, using any kind of material. Make it the size of a small beanbag and fill it with French chalk. By sweeping the bag over the paper, the static is removed. When you then sprinkle on the powder after having applied ink to the paper, the powder will cling only to those bits where ink is present. Therefore there won't be grains of powder all over the place.

Always remember to finish the embossing before pasting the photos on to the page. If heat is held close to the page it could damage your photos permanently.

REQUIREMENTS

- basic scrapbooking tools
- paper for embossing
- embossing stylus or embossing inkpad or pigment inkpad
- embossing powder
- heat source
- anti-static bag (optional)

Sweep the anti-static bag over the paper that is going to be embossed.

USING AN EMBOSSING STYLUS

1 Do the journalling or draw a picture on the paper, either freehand or with a stencil. Don't cover too large an area, as the ink must not dry before sprinkling the powder over it.

2 Sprinkle a little embossing powder over the inked sections. Tap the paper, and pour the remaining powder back into the container.

3 Heat the inked section. The powder will melt and take on a shiny, raised appearance.

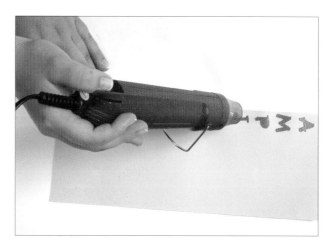

USING AN EMBOSSING INKPAD

1 The inkpad can be pressed on to the paper to make blocks, or a stamp can be used by pressing it on the inkpad and then on to the paper.

2 Next, follow steps 2 and 3 of 'Using an embossing stylus'.

USING A PIGMENT INKPAD

A pigment inkpad is used in exactly the same way as an embossing inkpad. Usually pigment ink takes longer to dry than other ink, but in this instance the pigment ink dries more quickly than the embossing ink; therefore work more quickly when sprinkling the powder on to the inked picture and heating it.

Complete the rest of the page by pasting the photo inside the frame. Don't forget to do the journalling and caption.

VARIATIONS

Cut out the embossed picture, mat it and use it as a decoration on your page.

Embossing can be done directly on to the background page and thus form a frame around a photo.

It can even form part of a picture on your page or create an entirely new one with a photo. The caption could also be embossed.

PHOTO CASCADE

This technique is very popular because you can fit a whole lot of photos on to one page. It's also an easy technique to master, since basically only cropping and pasting are done. What's more, this technique combines well with various other techniques such as mosaic work, Serendipity blocks and tearing.

There are eight pattern templates for photo cascades on pages 138–139. Each shape has two templates that are basically a mirror image of each other. The pasting line where the two templates must be joined together is also indicated. A circle, square, hexagon or octagon can be made. Adapt the shape of the photos or the technique you want to use to the template.

The width of a template is 10 cm. Feel free to make it bigger or smaller because the template as a whole doesn't fit on to an ordinary 12 x 12 inch (30.48 x 30.48 cm) scrapbook page; that's why it is cut in two and then joined again. The join lies along a fold so that it doesn't weaken the shape.

Make sure you position the photos correctly when you cut them out. Take note of where the photo is going to be pasted in the photo cascade, and which part of the shape must be at the top or at the bottom. This will prevent photos from accidentally being placed upside-down.

The front of the photo cascade can be decorated in various ways. For instance, use a photo, journalling or embellishments like punchies or tearing. Don't use raised decorations, as they will damage the plastic or even tear it.

Use a strong, acid-free, wet glue to stick the photo cascade to the page. Place your background page on a hard work surface in the spot where you have pasted the photo cascade. Then put something heavy on top of that to reinforce the pasting and also improve the folds of the cascade. Because wet glue is used and then a heavy object placed on top of it, the hard surface must be positioned between the background page and the back part of the album pocket. This prevents the glue from seeping through and damaging the back of the album pocket.

In this example I've made a square, but the directions can easily be adapted for the other shapes. Just substitute a square with a circle, hexagon or octagon; a triangle will then become a semicircle, semi hexagon or semi octagon. The only other difference between the square and all the other shapes is that the inside edges of the other shapes (the edges of shapes in the middle of the template) are not connected to the top and bottom edges of the adjacent shapes. The reason for this is to make sure that the photo cascade is able to fold up. The parts that have to be cut are clearly shown on the templates.

Remember, once the photo cascade has been pasted on to the page, it cannot be removed again from the pocket. Therefore make sure it is complete before reaching for the glue.

REQUIREMENTS

- basic scrapbooking tools
- thick cardboard, approximately
  12 x 12 cm
- thick or thin wadding, approximately
  12 x 12 cm
- polypropylene plastic, approximately
  15 x 15 cm (a torn album pocket will do)
- 2 plain sheets of paper (white works
  well, but you could use any colour as
  long as the paper's not too thin)
- 16–20 photos for the photo cascade
- 1 or 2 extra photos to complete the page
- 1 or more sheets of background paper
- 1 sheet of matching paper to complete
  the page
- craft knife
- a hard surface, small enough to fit into
  your album pocket, for you to press on
  when using the craft knife
- acid-free adhesive tape
- wet glue that adheres well

1 Cut one of each template from the plain paper. The two templates are basically a mirror image of each other.

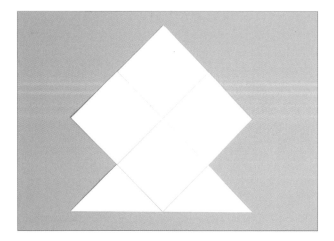

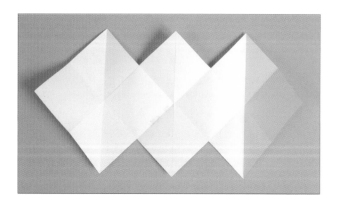

2 Crop the photos so that they fit into the shapes on the templates. They could also be cropped a little smaller so that a narrow paper frame is formed around the photos.

3 Before attaching the photos, the two templates must be pasted together. Use adhesive tape to stick the flat sides of the templates together (where photos 9, 10, 11 and 12 converge). Don't let the templates overlap. Just place them close together and stick them on both sides with adhesive tape.

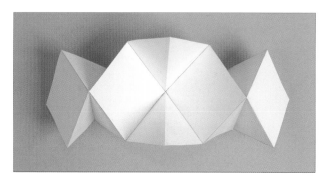

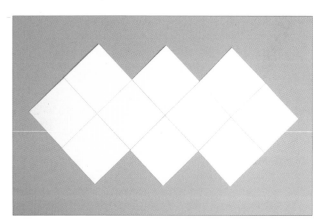

4 Now fold your templates on the folding lines so that the triangles fold towards each other. It may be a good idea to mark the folding line on the paper with a blunt razor blade, the back of a knife or opened-out scissors. This makes the fold neat and precise. Triangles 9, 10, 11 and 12 fold towards the back of the photo cascade, while the rest of the triangles fold towards the front.

5 Make sure the photo cascade works well and that all the folding lines fold easily. Stick adhesive tape along the fold lines to strengthen them. Now paste the photos into place.

6 Cut a 15 x 15 cm square from the matching paper you have chosen.

7 Place the square of wadding on the thick cardboard square. Now cover it with the paper you cut out in step 6. Cover the square again with the polypropylene plastic square.

8 Using strong wet glue, paste the back of the template (where photo number 1 is pasted) to the inside of this cardboard square.

9 Complete the rest of your page with the extra photos, captions and journalling. Leave the space open where you intend pasting the photo cascade.

10 Place the completed page into the album pocket and mark a 10 x 10 cm square on the plastic where the photo cascade will go.

11 Using the craft knife, cut the square from the plastic sleeve. Place a hard surface into the album pocket and press on it when you do the cutting.

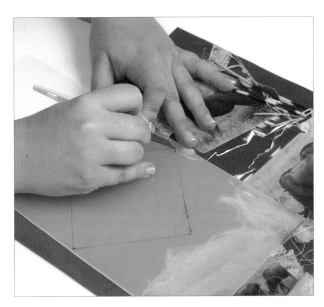

12 Now paste the photo cascade on the page in such a way that the back of your template, where photo number 4 is pasted, fits into the cutout square.

VARIATIONS

Here are a few examples of what the photo cascade looks like in the other shapes.

Another example of a square photo cascade

Circular photo cascade

Octagonal photo cascade. Here techniques such as Kaleidoscope, Serendipity and Crazy Mosaic were used to make the inside of the photo cascade more interesting.

Hexagonal photo cascade. Here Regular Mosaic was used on the inside of the cascade.

Make a foldout concertina book on which to paste photos. It can be attached to your page in the same way as explained on page 81, or even pasted on to the plastic pocket.

Concertina photo cascade

SCRAPPING WITH SERVIETTES

Serviettes are readily available and relatively cheap. They can be used as a background or as a focal point on your scrapbook page. In both instances an entire serviette can be pasted flat on to the background page. However, you can make your page look so much more special if the foam technique is used. When using a serviette as a background it will, unfortunately, have to be cropped, since most are larger than the 12 x 12 inch (30.48 x 30.48 cm) scrapbook pages. If the serviette has a nice border, it can be cut into quarters along the fold lines, and then cropped in the middle. The four quarters are then pasted separately on to the white background paper.

There are two techniques that need to be mastered when using the foam technique with serviettes: pasting the serviettes, and what to accentuate with the foam squares or move to the background.

Use a colourless glue stick to paste serviettes. Start by applying glue to a small area in the corner of the paper on which you want to paste the serviette. Always put glue on the paper and not on the serviette. Stick the serviette down, and fold back the area that has not been pasted down. Apply glue to another small area and stick down another part of the serviette. Continue doing this until the entire serviette has been pasted. The upper layer of the serviette will now become detached. Pull it off carefully and start pasting all over again. Spread the glue very carefully, since the already-pasted layer can easily tear and crumple.

Should your serviette accidentally tear, just put a little glue on to the background paper and paste it down again. You can't usually detect the fault once the project has been completed.

The easiest way to explain the foam technique is as follows: something far in the background is left as is while something in the foreground is brought forward/closer by using foam squares. Therefore a tree on the horizon would be left as is while a house in front of a hill would be lifted twice. A tree in front of the house would be lifted three times and a man standing in front of the tree, four times. In the case of a seated teddy bear, its head would probably be raised twice, its arms three times, and the soles of its feet four times.

In the example that follows, a serviette on which the picture is repeated twice will be used. I therefore need two serviettes. The serviette will only form a lower border on my background page, so I won't be using the entire serviette as a background.

REQUIREMENTS

• basic scrapbooking tools
• glue stick
• at least 2 or 3 serviettes with the same picture
• white paper for cutting up
• foam squares or strips
• paper for the background page

1 Pull off the back layer of the serviette and discard. Some serviettes have three layers, but only the top two are used so that the picture shows up at its brightest.

2 Cut out the background on the serviette. This could be the whole serviette or just the picture you want to use. This will be the largest part of the serviette you will be using as one piece; from here on in, you'll only be working with smaller pieces.

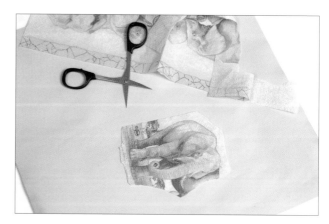

3 Paste the background part of the serviette on to the background paper. Use the pasting technique described in the introduction on page 85.

4 Cut out the smaller parts of the serviette that you want to raise – for instance, cut out each specific piece three times if you want to raise it three times, etc. There's no need to cut out the picture in detail, since you'll be pasting it on white paper and then cutting it out again. It's easier to cut paper than a limp serviette.

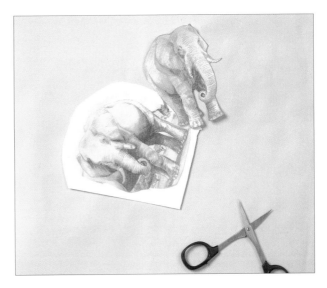

5 Paste these pieces on the white paper for cutting up. Again use the pasting technique and cut out neatly.

6 Paste foam squares on the back of all the cut-out pictures (the corresponding pictures you want to raise have already been pasted on to the background paper).

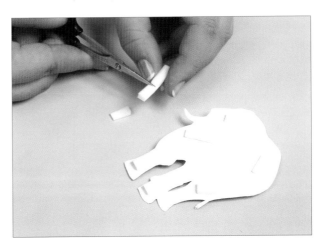

7 Complete the rest of the page by cropping and matting your photos and pasting them on to the background page. Don't forget to leave space for the caption and journalling.

VARIATIONS

Keep a serviette flat, in other words, don't use it three-dimensionally. Use it as a whole for the background page. Unfortunately, most serviettes are too big and must be cropped. Because most serviettes have a pretty border, I cut the serviettes into quarters and reduce them in the middle.

You needn't always use foam squares. Cut out pieces of the serviette and paste them as is on to the background page.

Have the entire serviette as a background, but lift out a few parts with foam squares.

Use part of the serviette to make a new picture or to form a frame on the background page.

Journalling

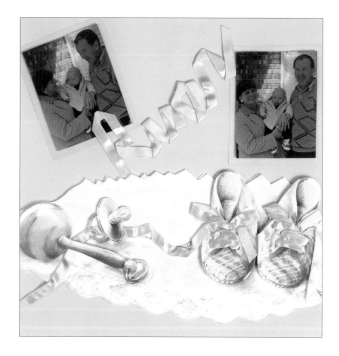

Combine the serviette with your photos in such a way that they form a new picture.

Use foam squares to help you imitate movement.

REGULAR MOSAIC

When doing regular mosaic, one works with straight horizontal and vertical lines. Therefore the squares must always be the same size. Should you wish to use double-length squares, the spaces between the photos must be taken into account so that the lines remain straight. Once again there are exceptions and it is possible to use varying square sizes, but then even more uneven spaces will have to be left open in which to do journalling, so that the lines are kept straight.

Glue that takes long to dry works well for mosaic, since a photo can be detached without difficulty and pasted in a different place. This glue is expensive, however, so simply use a photo split on each bit of photo. Don't press down too hard when you paste it so that it can easily be lifted if it is skew. When your page is complete, simply turn it over and apply pressure to the whole page so that all the squares are stuck down well.

REQUIREMENTS
- basic scrapbooking tools
- at least 4 standard-sized photos
- plain background paper
- craft knife
- a pair of scissors or a small guillotine
- photo pencil or light box

1 Crop all your photos into 2 x 2 cm squares. Adapt the size of the squares if you want to use larger or smaller photos. If you're using a pair of scissors you should use a photo pencil or light box to ensure that the lines are in the right place. If cropping with a guillotine, decide beforehand where you want the cutting lines to be, and then work with the guillotine's measurements.

2 Feel free to leave parts of the photos in bigger pieces. Calculate the size of a double-length square if the blocks are 2 x 2 cm. A double-length square will then be 2 x 4 cm. However, the space you intend leaving between the squares when you paste them must still be added, and this is usually a few millimetres. Therefore, cut each block approximately 2 x 4.3 cm. A square doubled in both width and length will therefore be 4.3 x 4.3 cm.

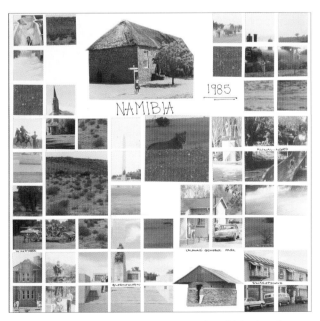

Here double-length squares were used and blocks of space were left for journalling

3 Paste each block in the shape of the original photo immediately after cutting, or number each square so that it makes it easier to assemble the 'jigsaw puzzle' with all the photo blocks later.

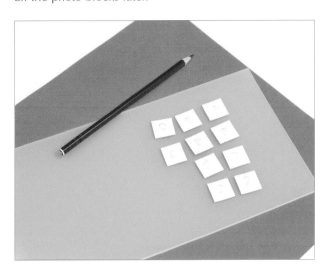

4 Attach each photo block to the background page using photo splits. Leave a space of a few millimetres between each block. Approximately 3 mm will do, but you could also leave a space of up to 8 mm or even 1 cm if that's what you prefer.

5 Keep pasting photos until your page is full.

6 Certain squares can be left out for you to do journalling in, or you could do your journalling in the spaces around the photo squares.

VARIATIONS

Regular mosaic can also be done by cutting the paper into squares or rectangles, thereby creating a new background for your photos.

Feel free to mix up your photos, thereby creating a new one. It will then look more like a picture than a number of photos pasted next to one another.

Use photos as frames. Make a few copies of a photo of pebbles and paste them along the edge of the page.

Make regular mosaic more interesting by keeping a photo intact, or silhouetting an object on a photo and not cutting it into squares. The correct way of doing this is arranging the squares that surround this silhouetted photo in such a way that they still retain the same frame width all around the silhouette. However, an easier way is to mat the silhouetted photo on the same

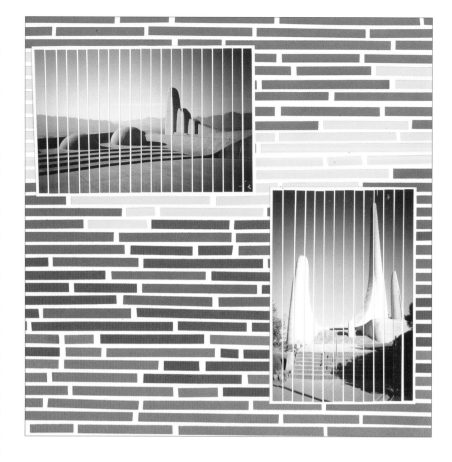

paper as the background paper. Ensure that the mat is the same width as the space between the squares. Then simply paste the silhouetted photo on to the photo blocks. In this way it will look as though the mosaic has been done correctly, but the process is much easier and usually looks better.

One needn't reshape the old photo with the squares at all; they can be used to form a frame around the background page instead.

Use only a small part of a photo and discard the rest. In this example, I cut out and used most of the faces, then discarded the rest of the photo.

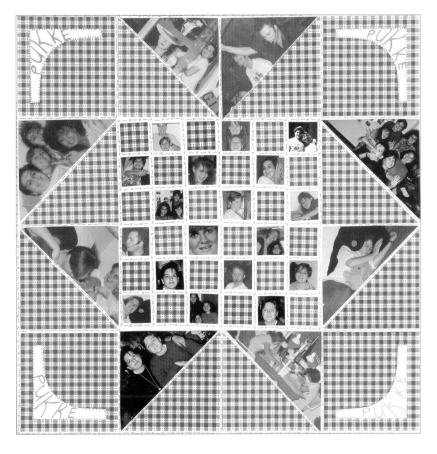

CRAZY MOSAIC

Crazy mosaic is based on regular mosaic and works well with angular shapes such as squares, oblongs and triangles, although you could also undertake a project using round shapes.

Photos are cut into many different shapes and sizes and the spaces in between filled up with crazy mosaic pieces. These can be cut from other photos and/or waste photos and/or the paper chosen to match the theme or colouring of the page.

REQUIREMENTS

- basic scrapbooking tools
- quite a large number of photos
- background paper
- a few sheets of matching paper (if you're not going to use photos only)
- tracing paper
- glue stick

1 Crop the photos so that only the most important parts are kept. They may be cropped into any shape, but squares or oblongs work well.

2 Cut the photos into pieces and, using photo splits, attach them to the background page. Leave spaces between the photos.

3 Fill the spaces with crazy mosaic pieces. Do this by laying tracing paper over the spaces and drawing crazy mosaic patterns in them. The spaces should not be too big, but if they are you could fill them with a few smaller mosaic patterns. Don't draw too many at a time, or you may become confused as to where each one must be pasted.

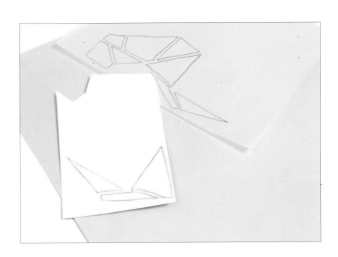

4 Use the waste photos you've cropped, the matching paper or extra photos as mosaic pieces. Using the glue stick, paste the tracing paper on to the back of the photo fragments or matching paper.

5 Cut out each mosaic pattern and paste it in its place in the space between the photos. Continue until all the empty spaces have been filled.

CRAZY D

This technique is based on crazy mosaic, but the end result resembles a broken mirror. Three or more copies are made of an enlarged photo. The first photo is cut into large pieces, the second one into slightly smaller pieces and the third photo into even smaller bits. Each piece is matted and arranged slightly askew onto the layer underneath, with uneven spaces left in between. Foam squares or strips used to paste the pieces create a three-dimensional effect.

REQUIREMENTS
- basic scrapbooking tools
- 3 or more copies of an enlarged photo
- background paper
- matching paper for matting
- foam squares or strips

1 Start with one photo and cut it into big pieces. Mat each piece.

2 Crop the second photo into slightly smaller pieces than the first one. Don't crop it on the same lines as the first photo. Mat each piece. Keep each photo's pieces in its own pile.

3 Now crop the third photo into the smallest pieces and mat each one.

4 Using photo splits, attach the pieces of the first photo to the background page. Leave uneven spaces between the pieces.

5 Paste the second photo on top of the first one on the background page. Use foam squares or strips to attach the pieces. Play with the spaces between the pieces and paste the bits slightly askew on to the first photo pieces to form a broken picture.

6 Continue in this way until all the layers of photos have been pasted. If you like, paste a photo piece where there is no photo fragment in the previous layer, paste two or more foam squares or strips on top of each other to acquire the right thickness. You needn't use all the photo pieces. The effect being created is that of a broken mirror. Remember to leave space for a caption and journalling.

MORE EXAMPLES

Here are two more examples of how this technique can be applied.

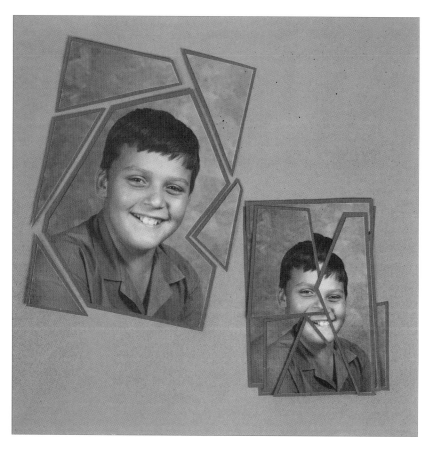

UPSIDE-DOWN 3-D

In this technique, I usually use three different-coloured sheets of paper. Parts of the upper sheet of paper are cropped to reveal the two sheets underneath. Smaller parts of the second sheet are then cut away, thereby revealing the bottom sheet. In other words, one needn't work with small bits of paper that have to be pasted in the right place to form a picture. The sheets of paper remain intact – patterns are cut away to reveal the other colours pasted underneath.

When drawing a picture, it's important to remember that all the parts of a single-coloured picture must touch one another. So if bits of the picture are cropped away, there should eventually be no loose bits that need to be pasted down. All the parts of the picture you want to retain must be attached somewhere to the greater part of the paper. This technique works well with three sheets of paper. In this example, however, I've used five sheets.

REQUIREMENTS
- basic scrapbooking tools
- photos
- light box (optional)
- at least 3 sheets of paper in various colours
- craft knife
- glue stick

Journalling

1 Use a light box or work against a window. Draw the part of the picture intended for the top page on the first sheet of coloured paper. Draw it again on the middle sheet(s). It's not necessary to draw it on the bottom sheet, since this page won't be cropped.

2 Using the craft knife, crop away those parts you don't want to use. Remember that the greater part of the top page is going to be cropped, while the middle page(s) will have smaller parts removed, and the bottom sheet won't be cropped at all.

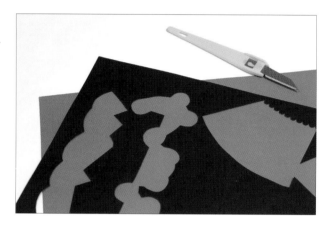

3 Using the glue stick, paste the different sheets of paper together from the bottom up.

4 You should now see a complete picture in the various colours as the middle and bottom pages show through the cut-out parts.

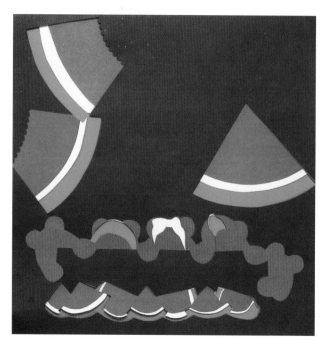

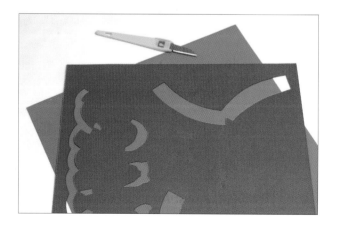

5 Complete the rest of the page by pasting down the photos. Don't forget to do journalling and a caption.

VARIATIONS

This method can also be used to make a frame around your photos.

An adaptation of this technique is to cut out the caption. Using foam squares, paste the paper from which the letters have been cut on to the background page or mat paper. Here I used the same paper for both layers. A shadow is created that makes the caption stand out.

In this example I adapted the technique a little. I cut the black paper so that the green and yellow would show through. Then I cut the green, so that the yellow would show through. Therefore the top layer was black, and then came the green and yellow layers. I then cut the picture from brown paper, the same paper I used for the background page, and pasted it on top of the black. The brown now forms a frame right around the cut-out parts and finishes off the picture.

FOAM WINDOWS

For this project foam paper is used. The benefit of foam paper sheets is that a large area can be lifted without having to use a lot of small foam squares or strips. The sheets are specially designed for scrapbooking and are obtainable from craft shops.

REQUIREMENTS
- basic scrapbooking tools
- 1 sheet of foam paper
- craft knife
- 2 sheets of paper in matching colours
- glue stick
- photo splits

1 Mark the windows to be cut from the foam paper.

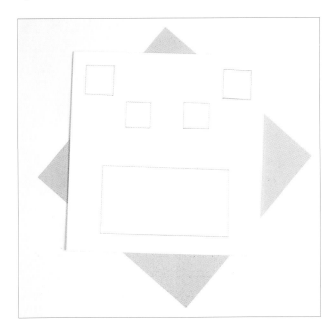

2 Using a craft knife, cut out each window.

3 Using the glue stick, paste one sheet of paper on to the foam paper.

4 There are two methods for this next step. Firstly, the paper can be cut about half a centimetre towards the inside of the window with the craft knife. In this case the album would have to be held at a slant to be able to see the white part of the foam paper in the window.

Secondly, diagonal slits can be cut in the corners of each window with the craft knife to form four triangles. The loose corners are then folded over and pasted on the back of the foam paper. The white sides of the foam paper are thus covered so that they aren't visible.

5 Place the foam paper precisely on to the other sheet of paper and lightly mark the windows. Remove and paste your photos on to the bottom page with photo splits.

6 Using the glue stick, paste the foam paper on to the bottom page.

7 Complete the rest of the page. Don't forget to do the journalling and caption.

PHOTO WEAVING

Photo weaving looks very impressive and is not nearly as complicated as it looks. Use a colour photo and a black and white copy of the same photo for your page. The same photo could also be taken twice – say, one in morning sun and the other in afternoon sun. You could also play around with the photos and use a predominantly blue and predominantly red copy of a photo. It's important, however, that it should be the same photo, whether you have a copy made or take the photo twice. Only one photo and a copy of this photo are therefore required per woven photo.

REQUIREMENTS
- basic scrapbooking tools
- 2 copies of a photo
- white paper for cutting up
- background paper

1 Mark the photo from top to bottom in 1 cm strips. Cut the photo and arrange the strips in sequence. If you're worried that the strips may become disarranged, number them on the back.

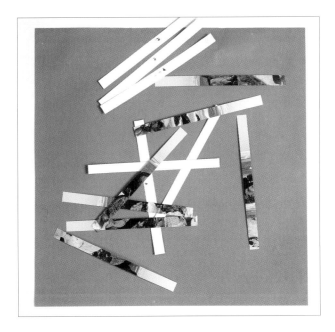

2 Mark the second photo in 1 cm strips from left to right. Once you've cut them out, trim about 1 mm off each side (now 8 mm wide). If these were the same width as the other strips, the photos would never fit on to each other precisely. Arrange the strips in sequence.

3 Paste the bottom left-hand corner of the first horizontal strip in the bottom left-hand corner of the white page. Don't apply glue to the whole strip, but only to the far left-hand side of the strip.

4 Place the next horizontal strip above the first strip. Do not paste.

5 Place the next horizontal strip above the second strip. Again, paste only the bit at the side. Carry on in this way until all the horizontal strips have been laid down in place on the white page.

6 Pull every second strip (those not pasted down) a little distance from the edge.

7 Now paste the left-hand **vertical** strip in place, **on top of the first, third and fifth horizontal strips**, and so on. Make sure that the entire strip is pasted down.

8 Paste the second, fourth, sixth and all the other **horizontal** strips in place **on to the left-hand vertical strip**. You have now formed the basis for photo weaving.

9 Weave in the rest of the vertical strips. First put glue on the edge of a strip and place it in position at the bottom of the page. Weave every second horizontal strip over that specific vertical strip. Carry on in this way until all the vertical strips have been woven in.

10 When weaving in the vertical strips, make sure that the picture on your photos coincides.

11 Carefully cut out the pasted photo from the white page it has been pasted on to. Paste this on to the background page. Cut a frame from matching paper to be pasted over the rough edges of the woven photo to finish it off.

12 Complete the rest of the page by adding journalling and a caption.

BARGELLO

Bargello is a folding technique by means of which various coloured or patterned paper strips are folded in half and pasted in a scrapbook in such a way that they form different patterns.

Feel free to score the paper strips in the middle so that they can be folded more easily. Craft shops sell special equipment for this, but I simply use a pair of scissors. Hold a ruler on the line where you want to score the paper. Open up the scissors completely and, using one of the scissor tips, score the line where the ruler is held. You have now made a clear folding line and can neatly fold the paper in half. When I fold the paper, I usually draw a line with a pencil and ruler down the middle of the back of the strip. I then fold the paper on the pencil line so that the front parts fold toward each other. The strip is then folded backwards.

Bargello strips can be pasted on to the background page to cover it completely (see the example in the variations on page 112), or they can be pasted on part of a page to make a frame around a photo or as an edge at the bottom of a page. Because folding and pasting paper are very simple to do, I have used a more advanced bargello technique for this project. Use the template on page 141 or create your own shapes.

REQUIREMENTS
- basic scrapbooking tools
- plain or patterned paper
- glue stick
- ruler
- background paper
- craft knife
- adhesive tape

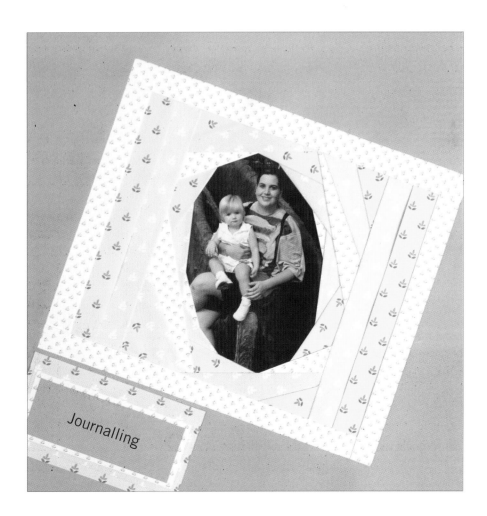

1 Draw a rectangle the same size as the template on the back of the background paper and cut it out with the craft knife.

2 Place the template in the window and stick it on to the background page with a small piece of adhesive tape. Set aside.

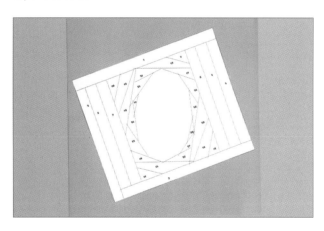

3 Choose the paper you wish to use and cut it into 4 cm strips. Fold each strip in half lengthways and paste closed.

4 Using the glue stick, paste the bargello strips on to the back of the background page. Start with number one. Use the guidelines on the template to show you where the bargello strips should be pasted. Make sure the fold line shows in front. Mark on the template where each strip should be used so that you don't become confused.

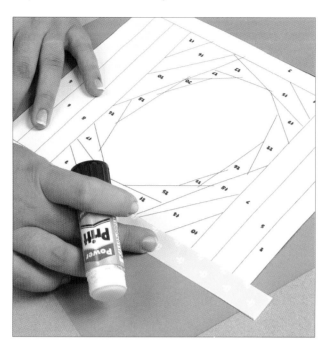

5 Continue in this way until all the paper strips have been pasted. Turn it over and carefully remove the template at the front.

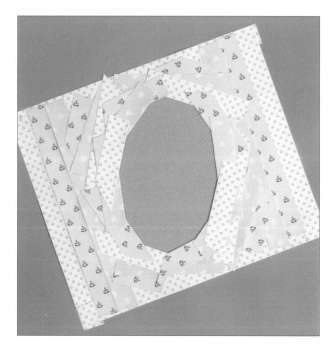

6 Turn it back and with the back facing you, paste the photo face down onto the back of the background page. Turn the page over again to see the result. You have now formed a frame of bargello strips around the photo. Complete the rest of the page.

VARIATIONS

You could also cut an oval window from the background page instead of a rectangle. This creates an interesting effect because the photo still forms a slightly slanted rectangle, the bargello strips form long thin triangles, and the outline of the window is an oval. Play around with other shapes as well.

The strips of paper are pasted in such a way that the folded edge always lies on top of the cut edges, thus producing a very neat end product. If you want to paste the strips diagonally across the entire background page, as in this example, the strips of paper won't be long enough. Mark the spot beforehand where you want your photo to be placed and paste the strips from that point outward. Draw diagonal lines as guides from corner to corner, so that the strips form a straight line.

Make the strips broader or narrower. In this case, 3 cm strips were folded in half to form bargello strips of 1.5 cm. The strips can be pasted on the background page any way you like. Of course, you needn't use only bargello strips. In this example I pasted grey paper strips to form three sections on the page. I also pasted some of the grey strips over the edges of the bargello strips to finish them off. The grey strips are not bargello strips because they have not been folded, but were used as is. I even pasted bargello strips over the grey strips to form a zigzag pattern. Play around with different ideas and create interesting new patterns.

POP-UP

This technique looks much more difficult than it is. Once you've mastered your first project, you'll want to try another page soon after. It looks impressive and makes your album interesting.

I like to use a strong, transparent, double-sided adhesive tape when I make pop-up pages. Photo splits also work well for pasting a pop-up on to your album pocket. Remember that the pop-up must be able to handle strain, because every time the album is opened the pop-up is pulled erect.

Any picture imaginable can be used to make a pop-up. Just remember that the pop-up shouldn't be too big. When the album is closed, the pop-up folds at a slant on the page. If it is too long, it will protrude from the sides of the album. If it's too big or too heavy, it will not stand up easily and could tear or become detached. The picture need not be symmetrical. The left- and right-hand sides may therefore differ from each other.

The album's thickness will determine how erect the pop-up will be. If the album is thick, the open pages will form a large curve. If the curve is too small, the pop-up will lean forwards. Solve the problem by adjusting the base of the pop-up accordingly. The greater the curve, the more aslant the fold of the pop-up base should be.

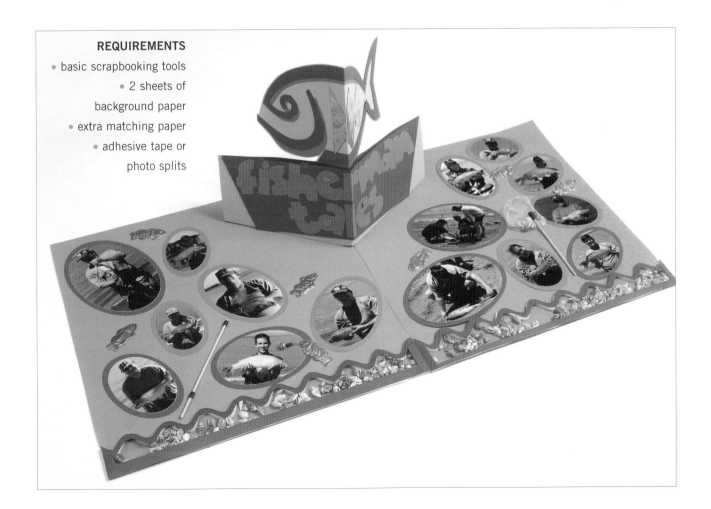

REQUIREMENTS
- basic scrapbooking tools
- 2 sheets of background paper
- extra matching paper
- adhesive tape or photo splits

1 Draw the template of the pop-up's base (page 141) on the matching paper. If necessary, adapt it as explained on page 113. Draw the pop-up picture above the base.

2 Cut out the picture and base as one. Fold the pop-up on the base's folding line.

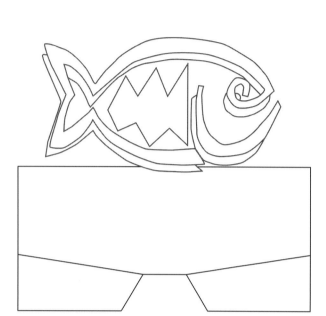

3 Complete the rest of your scrapbook pages. Crop, mat and paste your photos. Also do the journalling and captions. Leave open the middle top part of the double-page spread where the pop-up will be attached.

4 Put sufficient photo splits or double-sided adhesive tape on the bottom of the pop-up base. Remove the protective paper layer. Fold up the pop-up and stick one side lightly to the album pocket. Close the album and press down on it lightly. Open it again carefully. The pop-up should now be stuck in the right place, and have the correct angle so that it can be pulled erect and folded up easily. If it is not in the correct place, carefully detach it and move it slightly. Repeat until the pop-up is fixed in the right place.

VARIATION

For variation, more than one pop-up per page can be made.

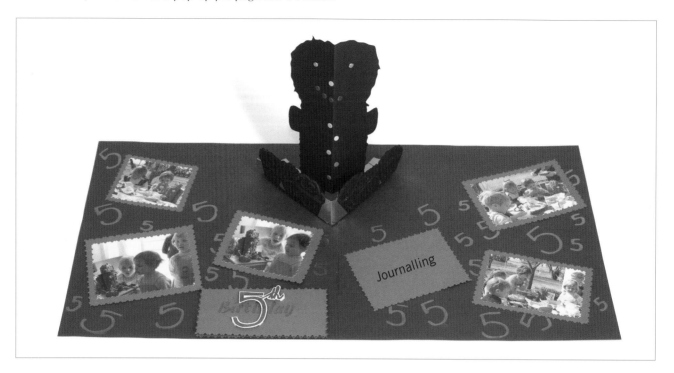

In this example, more than one technique was used. I made a simple pop-up, then added hide-and-seek forms. These are extra pages attached to the top edge of the album pocket, which open out to display what's underneath. I usually attach these forms to the pocket and background page with eyelets. Just remember to finish the background page completely before attaching the top page, since the background page can't be removed from the pocket again.

ADVANCED PHOTO POP-UP

I would recommend that you first make a few ordinary pop-up pages before undertaking this more advanced technique. Here the photo pop-up constitutes the largest part of the photo and there is little room left on the page for scrapbooking. Always remember that the photos should be the central point of the page and shouldn't disappear among all the embellishments.

There's not much difference between ordinary pop-up work and a photo pop-up. However, keep a cool head, because you'll be working with heavier, multiple pop-ups on one page.

Don't decide too far in advance which photos you want to paste where. It's easier to build up the picture as you go along than to plan the page in its entirety before you begin.

Because photos are heavy, it's better to use thicker paper for the pop-up base. I usually use white paper and, when I make a large pop-up, I fortify the paper by sticking two sheets together. You could also stick thick cardboard on to the back of the pop-up to strengthen it and make it stand erect.

Don't put more than four layers of pop-ups on to one page. All the layers must be made at the same time because in this way the picture develops more effectively. For the second and third pop-ups, the pasting line will be moved up higher and higher. In this way a pavilion effect is created, which helps one to see the photos at the back quite easily. Therefore each pop-up on the page doesn't stand on its own, but together with the others forms part of a new picture.

As the pasting line of the back pop-up becomes higher, the length of the pop-up becomes shorter. The reason for this is simply the availability of space on the page. The lower down on the page the pop-up is attached, the longer its sides can be.

It usually works best when the photos are silhouetted. Also use parts of the photo that you would normally have thrown away, such as cars in the foreground, signposts, streetlamps, etc.

Use larger photos for the pop-up at the back. In doing so, the photos will still be visible. It should be like a class photo – you should be able to see all the faces.

REQUIREMENTS

- basic scrapbooking tools
- 2 sheets of background paper
- firm matching paper for the pop-up base
- photos
- photo splits
- double-sided adhesive tape or strong dry glue
- cardboard strips for reinforcement if a heavy pop-up is to be made

1 Draw the template of the pop-up base (page 141) on the firm matching paper. Adapt as required.

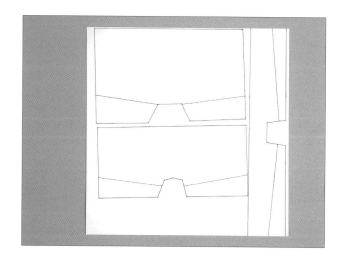

2 Draw another line above the base's folding line, about 5–8 cm above – this is the part on which the photos will be pasted.

3 Also draw the other pop-up bases you'll be needing. Lengthen their pasting lines and shorten their side lengths as required.

4 Cut out. Fold the pop-up along the base's folding line.

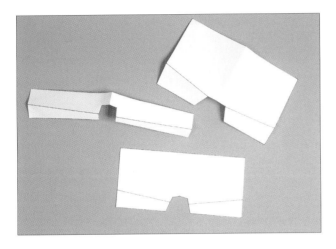

5 Cut out the photos. Now build the picture by pasting the photos on to the various pop-up bases. Use photo splits to attach the photos. Move the photos up higher from the pop-up base on the middle pop-up and even higher on the back one. This ensures that all the photos will be visible when the bases are in position.

6 Complete the rest of each page. Crop, mat and paste the photos. Also do the journalling and captions. Leave open the greater part of the pages where the pop-ups will be attached.

7 Stick the pop-ups to the album pocket. Leave open a 1.5–2.5 cm space between the pop-up layers. Start with the back pop-up and work towards the front.

8 If your pop-up is too heavy or too big to stand erect, it should be fortified on the back. Cut strips from thick cardboard and paste them vertically or diagonally on to the back of the pop-up.

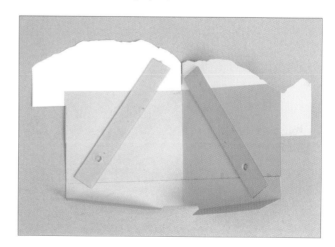

VARIATIONS

Here is another example of an advanced photo pop-up.

Move your pop-up so that one side forms a V and the other side an upside-down V on your page. In this way a little camp is formed.

I call this technique the concertina pop-up technique. Use a card or fold an oblong piece of paper in half to form a card. Now fold another piece of paper like a concertina and paste the bottom part on to the inside of the card, and the upper side of the concertina to the inside top part of the card. When the card is opened, the concertina forms an arch over the fold in the card. Paste photos or embellishments in the folds of the concertina. These will stand up when the card is opened. Paste the card on to the background page. Cut a little flap in the album pocket according to the size of the card. Paste the flap on to the top of the card. In this way the card can be opened and the top is protected.

Experiment with folding pop-ups. In this example I made the name Pretoria fold to a different side than of the rest of the pop-up. Cut a gap between the bottom part that folds backwards and the top part that folds forwards. Reinforce the Pretoria part by pasting cardboard strips on to the back of the paper. The pop-up must be strong enough to stand upright.

All six cards on this page are concertina pop-ups. I lengthened the page on both sides by cropping the album pocket and pasting it on to the side of the page with adhesive tape. Both sides open out to show another two three-dimensional techniques. The one needs two or three of the same photo, of which parts are raised by using foam squares. (See scrapping with serviettes pages 85–91.) The other technique is folding the photo in half and attaching one side to an extra insert of paper that works like a card, and the other to the part that opens out. In this way the photo stands up when the flap is opened.

SHAKER BOXES

A shaker box is a flat, paper box with a transparent window through which small, loose items can be seen inside the box. Shaker boxes can be made in any shape imaginable – a rattle for a page about a new baby, a golf bag for a page on Dad's hobby, waves for sea photos or a drop of water for a swimming pool party, or even the letters of a caption.

Almost any conceivable, dry filling can be used, from sand for a page about the sea to little shells and pebbles. Use glitter or sequins for a page about a gala evening, a concert or a little girl in a fairy dress. You could also use punchies that suit the theme of the page: little frogs and lizards for a page about a boy; bunnies and eggs for Easter; Christmas trees and Santa Clauses for Christmas photos. Buttons, confetti or rose petals can also be used. The possibilities are endless. Stick the boxes down with foam squares or strips. If you're making a complicated design, like the letters of the caption, it's easier to use squares than strips. Strips work well for simple designs. It's very important that the foam squares or strips slot closely together, so that the filling can't fall out.

Shaker box fillings usually stand out better when the shaker box has a plain paper background. Therefore, if you're using a patterned background for your page, it's a good idea to detach the shaker box so that you can give it a plain background. If you want to use the same background for both, a fixed shaker box can be made.

Once the box has been made, it needs to be finished off with a frame. This also hides the foam squares or strips. The frame can be made from plain or patterned paper and decorated with, among other things, punchies or journalling; or it could be cut out with pinking shears. You could, of course, make a square or oblong shaker box and make the frame a different shape. If you do this, you must bear in mind that the shaker box should not be much bigger than the window that peeps out from under the frame, or the filling in the box will be hidden beneath it.

Even the letters of a caption can be shaker boxes

REQUIREMENTS
- plain paper
- foam squares or strips
- plastic film (transparency or torn album pocket)
- filling for the box, for example confetti

1 Select the photos for your project. Remember to leave room for the box, so don't cram too many photos on to one page. Crop and mat the photos as preferred.

2 Cut the foam strips lengthwise. Paste them along the edges of the plain paper shapes. Don't remove the protective layer of the foam strips just yet. Make sure that the strips are very close together.

3 Put the filling into the box. Make sure the filling cannot spill from the sides. If there's a gap it can fall through, cut a small foam strip and stick it into the gap.

2 Select the shape of the box.

LOOSE SHAKER BOX

1 Cut the shape of the shaker box from the plain paper. It should be about 1 cm bigger than the eventual inside of the box. Cut the same shape from the plastic film.

4 Gently remove the protective layer from the foam strips with a pair of tweezers. Stick the plastic shape on top.

5 Finish the box off neatly by making a frame approximately 1 cm wider. Using a craft knife, cut out the inside of the frame. Stick the frame on to the plastic film with the glue stick and decorate.

6 Stick the box on to the page with photo splits. Complete the rest of the page by pasting in the photos and adding the caption or journalling.

FIXED SHAKER BOX

1 Trace the shape of the shaker box on to the background paper in the spot where you want it to be attached. Cut a similar-sized shape from the plastic film.

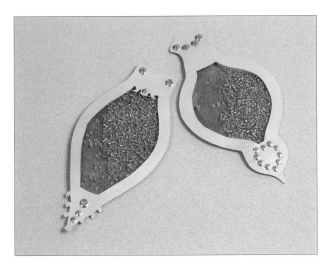

2 Stick the foam squares along the edge of the shape on the background page.

3 Pour in the filling, remove the protective layer from the foam squares and stick the plastic shape on top. Finish off the box by making a frame and sticking it onto the box.

4 Complete the rest of the page by cropping and matting your photos and then pasting them on to the background page. Don't forget to leave room for the caption and journalling.

PARCHMENT ART

Parchment art is inkwork, embossing and piercing on thick parchment or vellum paper whereby delicate lace patterns are formed. It combines very well with scrapbooking and because it's an art form in its own right, I will only touch on a few basic points. When working with parchment, one needs special equipment. There are styli available with two tips, three tips in a row, three tips that form a triangle, and so on. For the simple parchment art discussed here, you'll need a single-tipped stylus. See the section on parchment art equipment on page 18.

Parchment art has three phases. Firstly a pattern is drawn on parchment paper using white ink and a calligraphy pen. Parchment paper is most commonly used, but for variation I have also used ordinary metallic paper (see example below). This gives one the feeling of working with parchment, although the end product is not white on white. Craft shops also stock various parchment ink colours so you needn't work with white ink only.

Secondly, the dry embossing (see pages 72–73) is done. Parchment paper is ideal for dry embossing because the paper turns white when stretched by the pressure of the embossing. In the example on page 129 (top left) I drew only the lines in white ink. The inside is raised by the dry embossing and, because of the paper stretching, it looks as though it has been coloured in white.

Thirdly, holes are pierced evenly into the paper with the stylus, so that the paper is eventually cut. The holes form patterns that look like lace. These holes needn't always cut the paper and can serve as a delicate adornment. In the heart example on the opposite page (top right), every second heart not coloured in has been decorated with holes. See also the four holes in each diamond and the two lines of holes in the frame of each heart.

Embossing causes parchment paper to turn white

Every second heart as well as the diamonds and heart frames have been decorated with piercing

REQUIREMENTS

- basic scrapbooking tools
- parchment art equipment
- round-tipped embossing stylus
- wax
- transparent vellum splits
- paper

1 Using white ink, trace the picture on to your parchment paper.

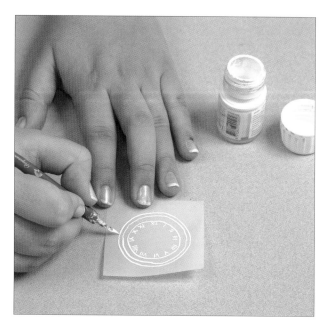

2 Using the round-tipped embossing stylus, exert light pressure on the back of the page on those parts you want to raise and show up as white. Every now and then dip the tip of the stylus into the wax to allow the stylus to glide over the page more smoothly.

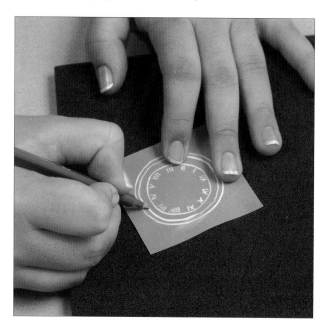

3 Using the stylus, evenly press holes all along the line. In places where you want to cut the paper, the holes need to be very close together. In places where the holes only serve as a decoration, they can be a little further apart.

4 Use transparent vellum splits to stick the parchment decoration to the background page.

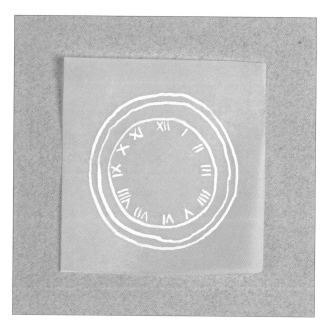

5 Complete the rest of the page. Don't forget about the journalling and caption.

QUILLING

Quilling is the art of winding paper strips into spools, which are used to make pictures and frames. Quilling is also an art form in its own right, so once again I will only be explaining a few basic techniques for when they are applied to scrapbooking.

When you do quilling, you'll need a pen that has a steel nib with a groove in the middle. You'll also need narrow strips of paper. These strips can be purchased at craft shops in a variety of colours and widths. Of course, you could also cut your own strips. Put the end of the paper strip into the pen's groove and wind the paper around the steel nib. The length of the paper strip will determine the size of the wound-up paper spool. When removing the spool of paper from the steel nib, the shape of the spool can be manoeuvred with your index finger and thumb. Instead of a round spool, a diamond, oval, half-moon, eyelet or any other shape can be created. The paper spools are simply pasted on to your page with wet glue to make pictures, frames etc.

Both closed and open paper spools can be made. Closed spools are the most common – the outermost strip is pasted on to the paper spool. Once it has been pasted down, the spool can be shaped. In the case of open spools, the outermost strip is simply left detached after removing it from the pen. It is normally used as a decoration around a picture.

In the example that follows, I have made a decoration. My paper strips are approximately 2 mm wide, but wider strips can also be used. If you enjoy quilling, it may be a good idea to buy a book on the craft. You'll be amazed at how much can be done with just a few paper strips.

REQUIREMENTS

- basic scrapbooking tools
- paper strips in various colours
- wet glue
- quilling pen
- ruler
- paper

Use the following lengths and colours for the various patterns on the decoration:

BIG FISH

i)   30 cm purple for the body and tail
ii) 8 cm lilac for the upper fin
iii) 6 cm lilac for the lower fin
iv) 6 cm red for the mouth

SMALL FISH

i)   20 cm purple for the body
ii) 10 cm lilac for the tail
iii) 5 cm red for the mouth
iv) two 5-cm strips of lilac for the upper and lower fins

BIRD

i)   25 cm beige for the body
ii)   10 cm beige for the head
iii) 5 cm orange for the beak
iv)   two 5-cm strips of orange for the feet
v)   15 cm dark beige for the wing
vi)   10 cm dark beige for the tail
vii) two 1.5-cm strips of orange for the legs
viii) 2 cm dark beige for the neck

WATER

i)   two 8-cm strips of dark blue and two of light blue
ii) two 4-cm strips of dark blue and two of light blue
iii) 6 cm dark blue and 6 cm light blue

FISHING ROD

i)   6 cm dark brown for the rod
ii) 5 cm white for the line

FROG WITH JOURNALLING

i)   20 cm dark blue for the body
ii) 20 cm dark blue for the head
iii) 20 cm dull blue for the head
iv) two 10-cm strips of dull blue for the legs
v)   two 15-cm strips of light blue for the feet
vi) two 20-cm strips off-white for the eyes and the 'oo' in Dullstroom

1 Put the end of the paper strip into the pen's groove.

2 Wind the paper strips around the steel nib and remove the paper spools. Stick the end of each respective paper spool down to form a closed spool.

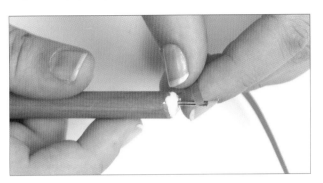

3 Using your index finger and thumb, squeeze the paper spools and manipulate them into the following shapes:

BIG FISH

i) **body and tail** – press on the one side to make a slight point where the mouth will be. About three-quarters into the body, press the ends towards each other to form two parts. The small part forms the tail. Press this part into a triangle.

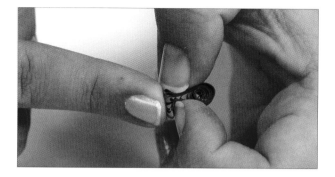

ii) **upper fin** – press into a triangle with one flat side a little toward the inside to form a curve. This curve comes right up against the body.

iii) **lower fin** – the same as for the upper fin.

iv) **mouth** – press in a groove to form two lips.

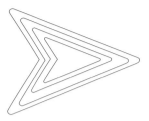

SMALL FISH

i) **body** – make a teardrop shape.

ii) **tail** – make a triangle.

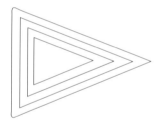

iii) **upper and lower fin** – the same as for the big fish.

iv) **mouth** – the same as for the big fish.

BIRD

i) **body** – make a teardrop shape.

ii) **head** – make the eyes by simply pressing lightly on either side.

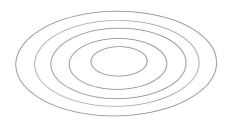

iii) **beak** – make an acute-angled triangle.

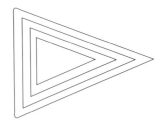

iv) **feet** – the same as for the mouth of the big fish.
v) **wing** – the same as for the body.
vi) **tail** – make a triangle.
vii) **legs** – fold in half.

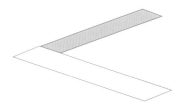

viii) **neck** – the same as for the legs.

WATER

Shape waves with paper strips. Weave the dark and light blues together so that they move up and down in the same place. If you want them to look different, twist each colour separately. Where the line passes through the water, simply cut a notch in the strips once they have been pasted down.

FISHING-ROD

i) **rod** – the same as the bird's legs and neck.
ii) **line** – the same as the water.

FROG WITH JOURNALLING

i) **body** – press one side slightly flatter to form a round body with a flat side.

ii) **head** – flatten to form a flat oval; roll around the top part of the head to increase the size of the head (this is to form an outside oval around the inside one).
iii) **legs** – press flat to form a flat oval.
iv) **feet** – hold a piece tightly and then press on both sides of the paper to form three toes. When you have shaped the three toes, hold them tightly and then form the rest of the spool into a triangle.

v) **eyes and the 'oo' of Dullstroom** – keep round.

4 Cut out a tag from your scrapbook paper. Using a little wet glue, stick the paper spools on to the tag. Use this tag as an embellishment on your album page.

5 Complete the rest of the page. Don't forget to do the journalling and caption.

VARIATIONS

Wind one side of the paper strip until almost in the middle around the steel nib. Remove it from the pen and, starting from the other end, again wind it to almost in the middle. Remove. This forms two spools that either face each other or look away from each other, depending on the direction in which you have wound them. The yellow paper spools on the outside of the circles were made in this way. For the candle flame, I wound the same lengths of yellow and orange paper strips together.

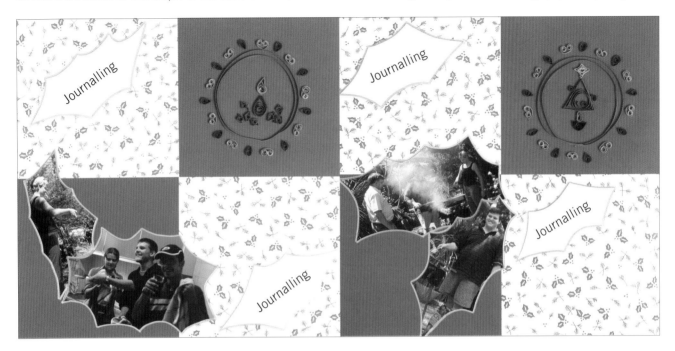

Quilling spools can also be pasted directly on to your background page to form a picture or a frame around a photo. See the different items I made with quilling spools to demonstrate the wares available at a market in Mauritius (right).

TEMPLATES

PHOTO CASCADES (PAGES 78–84)

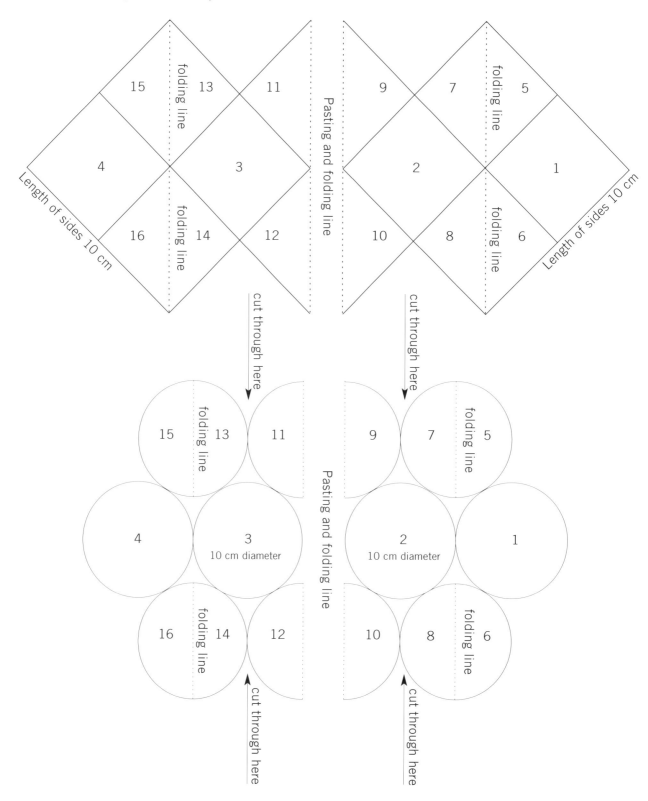

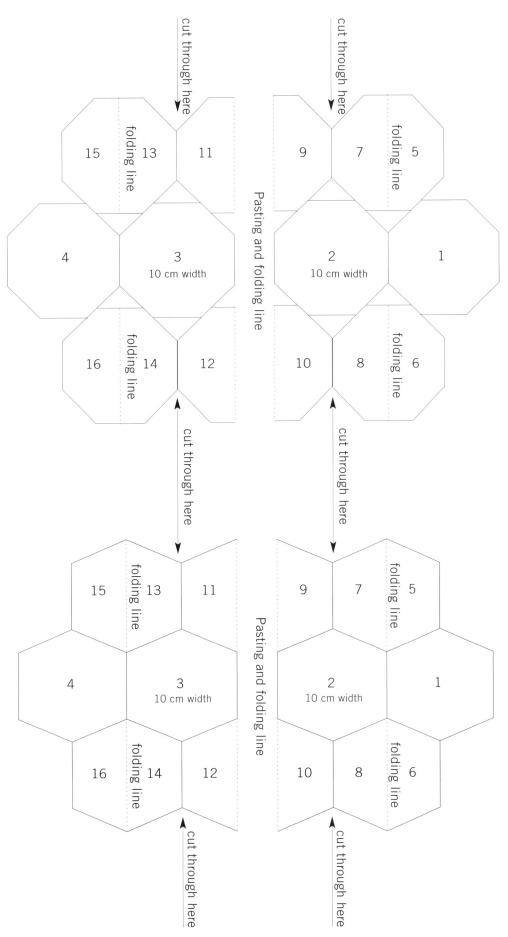

cut through here

folding line

15 13 11

4 3
10 cm width

16 14 12

folding line

Pasting and folding line

cut through here

cut through here

folding line

9 7 5

2 1
10 cm width

10 8 6

folding line

cut through here

folding line

15 13 11

4 3
10 cm width

16 14 12

folding line

Pasting and folding line

cut through here

folding line

9 7 5

2 1
10 cm width

10 8 6

folding line

cut through here

VARIOUS SHAPES FOR PHOTO CASCADES (PAGES 78–84)

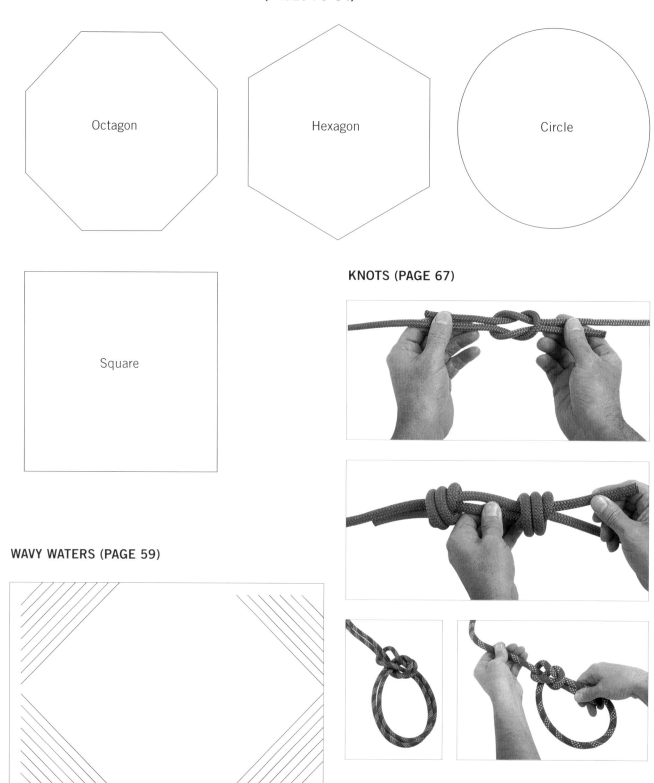

Octagon

Hexagon

Circle

Square

KNOTS (PAGE 67)

WAVY WATERS (PAGE 59)

BARGELLO (PAGE 109)

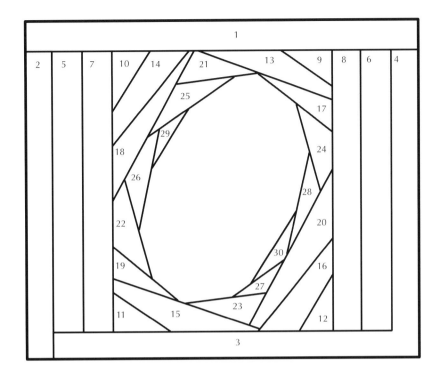

PHOTO POP-UPS (PAGES 113–123)

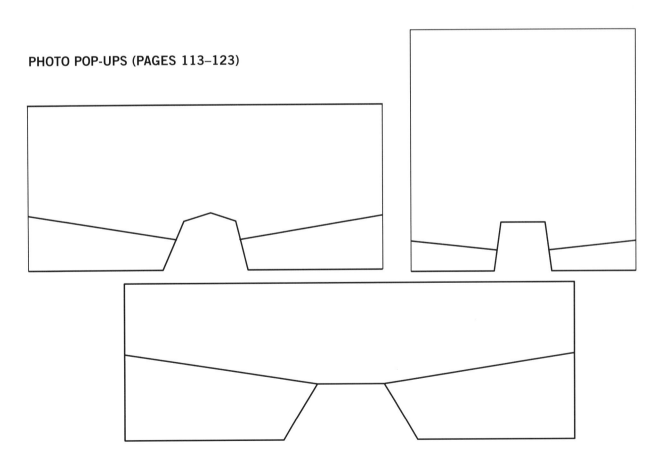

SUPPLIER'S LIST

WESTERN CAPE

Crafty Supplies
74 Loch Road
Claremont
CAPE TOWN
Tel: 021 671 0286
Fax: 021 671 0308

Scrapbook Den
2 Blue Valley Avenue
Hout Bay
CAPE TOWN
Tel/fax: 021 790 0944
E-mail: addisons@bucknet.co.za

The Scrapbook
14 Kowie Road
Mowbray
CAPE TOWN
Tel: 021 689 6738
E-mail: info@thescrapbook.co.za

The Scrapbox
De Bron
12 Ongegund Street
Bellville
CAPE TOWN
Tel: 021 913 8492

EASTERN CAPE

The Scrapbook Nook
152 Main Road
Walmer
PORT ELIZABETH
Tel: 041 581 4514
Fax: 041 581 5550
E-mail: pippadyson@mweb.co.za

KWAZULU-NATAL

Scrapbooking
6 Heath Place
Northdene
DURBAN
Tel: 031 708 1588/083 656 0685

The Scrapbook Inn
692 Stella Road
Escombe
DURBAN
Tel 031 464 1722/082 374 355

GAUTENG

Creative Talents*
Crafters Warehouse
Units 4–7
5 Harrington Road
Duncanville
VEREENIGING
Tel: 016 427 1030
Fax: 016 427 1031
*Also branches in Witbank, the East
    Rand, Klerksdorp and Umhlanga

Garing en Goed
Magalieskruin Centre
c/o Gryshout & Braam
    Pretorius Streets
Magalieskruin
PRETORIA
Tel: 012 543 0553

Scrapaholics
163 Leeupoort Street
BOKSBURG
Tel: 011 917 0890/083 381 0945

Scrap'n 4 Africa
Shop 10, Parkmore Mews
c/o 11th & Olympic Avenues
SANDTON
Tel: 011 883 4696

Sweet Scrappin's
c/o 24th Avenue & Pierneef Street
Villieria
PRETORIA
Tel/fax: 012 329 9175

The Scrapbook
Shop 68
Heathway Square
Beyers Naudé Drive
BLACKHEATH
Tel: 011 476 8600
info@thescrapbook.co.za

NOTE

The author and publishers have made every effort to ensure that all instructions given in this book are safe and accurate, but they cannot accept liability for any resulting injury or loss or damage to either property or person, whether direct or consequential and howsoever arising.

INDEX

AUTHOR'S ACKNOWLEDGEMENTS

It takes so much more than I originally imagined to get a book, at first simply an idea, onto the shelves. I therefore feel obliged to thank a few people for their help and support.

Firstly, thank you very much to Struik Publishers and the people I worked with who provided friendly, professional service throughout.

My thanks also go to Karen Sterley from *Garing en Goed* in Pretoria for her friendship and advice. If it weren't for her shop, I would never have become involved in scrapbooking to begin with. I also appreciate the fact that she always went to so much trouble to track down products I couldn't find anywhere else.

To everyone who does scrapbooking – all of you who follow and enjoy this hobby; everyone I meet at workshops and craft stores; those from whom I constantly learn new techniques and get great ideas; and all who faithfully attend my classes every month – you have all become true friends.

My family and friends also deserve my thanks. My parents and parents-in-law for their advice and support; my mum, mother- and sister-in-law who have all been bitten by the scrapbooking bug and spend hours doing this hobby with me; and my friends for their interest in the progress of the book. To my husband, Gerrit, thank you for your involvement and ongoing faith in me, and for listening to my constant chatter about the book and scrapbooking in general. Thanks, too, for your advice and for bringing my ideas to life with your creative devices.

Without everyone's support it would have been an arduous task getting this book published.

Lastly, I humbly place myself and this book in God's hands, because without Him I am incapable of doing anything.

This edition produced for
The Book People Ltd
Hall Wood Avenue
Haydock
St Helens WA11 9UL

First published in 2005 by Struik Publishers (a division of New Holland Publishing (South Africa) (Pty) Ltd)
Cornelis Struik House, 80 McKenzie Street, Cape Town 8001
New Holland Publishing is a member of Johnnic Communications Ltd
86–88 Edgware Road, London, W2 2EA, United Kingdom
14 Aquatic Drive, Frenchs Forest, NSW 2086, Australia
218 Lake Road, Northcote, Auckland, New Zealand

www.struik.co.za

PUBLISHING MANAGER: Linda de Villiers
MANAGING EDITOR: Cecilia Barfield
EDITOR: Irma van Wyk
DESIGNER: Beverley Dodd
PHOTOGRAPHER: Sean Nel
ILLUSTRATOR: Janine Cloete
PROOFREADER: Joy Clack

Translated into English by Sylvia Grobbelaar from *Skep Jou Eie Fotoplakboek*

Reproduction by Hirt & Carter Cape (Pty) Ltd
Printed and bound by Kyodo Printing Co (Singapore) Pte Ltd

ISBN 1 77007 023 0

10 9 8 7 6 5 4 3 2

www.imagesofafrica.co.za

IMAGES OF AFRICA
PHOTO LIBRARY